PSYCHOLOGY OF EMOTIONS, MOTIVATIONS AND
ACTIONS SERIES

THE PSYCHOLOGY OF PESSIMISM

PSYCHOLOGY OF EMOTIONS, MOTIVATIONS AND ACTIONS SERIES

Psychology of Aggression
James P. Morgan (Editor)
2004. ISBN 1-59454-136-1 (Flexback)

New Research on the Psychology of Fear
Paul L. Gower (Editor)
2005. ISBN: 1-59454-334-8

Impulsivity: Causes, Control and Disorders
George H. Lassiter (Editor)
2009. ISBN: 978-60741-951-8

Handbook of Stress: Causes, Effects and Control
Pascal Heidenreich and Isidor Prüter (Editors)
2009. ISBN: 978-1-60741-858-0

Handbook of Aggressive Behavior Research
Caitriona Quin and Scott Tawse (Editors)
2009. ISBN: 978-1-60741-583-1

Psychology of Happiness
Anna Mäkinen and Paul Hájek (Editors)
2010. ISBN: 978-1-60876-555-3

The Psychology of Pessimism
Daniel X. Choi; Ravi B. DeSilva and John R. T. Monson
2010. ISBN: 978-1-60876-802-8

PSYCHOLOGY OF EMOTIONS, MOTIVATIONS AND
ACTIONS SERIES

THE PSYCHOLOGY OF PESSIMISM

DISCARD

DANIEL X. CHOI
RAVI B. DESILVA
AND
JOHN R. T. MONSON

Nova Science Publishers, Inc.
New York

Copyright © 2010 by Nova Science Publishers, Inc.

For permission to use material from this book please contact us:
Telephone 631-231-7269; Fax 631-231-8175
Web Site: http://www.novapublishers.com

NOTICE TO THE READER

The Publisher has taken reasonable care in the preparation of this book, but makes no expressed or implied warranty of any kind and assumes no responsibility for any errors or omissions. No liability is assumed for incidental or consequential damages in connection with or arising out of information contained in this book. The Publisher shall not be liable for any special, consequential, or exemplary damages resulting, in whole or in part, from the readers' use of, or reliance upon, this material.

Independent verification should be sought for any data, advice or recommendations contained in this book. In addition, no responsibility is assumed by the publisher for any injury and/or damage to persons or property arising from any methods, products, instructions, ideas or otherwise contained in this publication.

This publication is designed to provide accurate and authoritative information with regard to the subject matter covered herein. It is sold with the clear understanding that the Publisher is not engaged in rendering legal or any other professional services. If legal or any other expert assistance is required, the services of a competent person should be sought. FROM A DECLARATION OF PARTICIPANTS JOINTLY ADOPTED BY A COMMITTEE OF THE AMERICAN BAR ASSOCIATION AND A COMMITTEE OF PUBLISHERS.

LIBRARY OF CONGRESS CATALOGING-IN-PUBLICATION DATA

Choi, Daniel X.
  The psychology of pessimism / Daniel X. Choi, Ravi B. DeSilva, John R. T. Monson.
    p. cm.
  Includes index.
  ISBN 978-1-60876-802-8 (softcover)
  1. Pessimism. 2. Health. I. DeSilva, Ravi B. II. Monson, John R. T. III. Title.
  BF698.35.P49C46 2010
  150.19--dc22
                          2009048927

Published by Nova Science Publishers, Inc. + *New York*

CONTENTS

PREFACE

For various reasons, rigorous analysis of pessimism has been difficult. Nonetheless, recent advances, including the development of numerous psychological batteries, have allowed for structured, scientific investigation. Indeed, several studies have examined the medical implications and biological and chemical bases of pessimism. Nonetheless, the psychology of pessimism is imperfect and further study is needed.

INTRODUCTION

Optimism and pessimism are complementary, but opposing, dispositions. In general, optimists consistently expect good outcomes and pessimists consistently expect bad outcomes. These variations in human behavior have profound mental and physical implications.

The aim of the present work is to provide an overview of the psychology of pessimism. It is composed of four sections – I: How are optimism and pessimism measured?, II: What is the relationship between optimism and pessimism?, III: What is the relationship between optimism-pessimism and health?, and IV: What are the biology and chemistry of optimism-pessimism?

I: HOW ARE OPTIMISM AND PESSIMISM MEASURED?

The *Diagnostic and Statistical Manual of Mental Disorders, 4th Edition, Text Revision* [DSM-IV-TR] is the working manual of the mental-health professions.[1] It catalogs 297 psychiatric disorders and their diagnostic criteria, and has proven useful to both clinicians and researchers. However, despite its ubiquitous use and good intentions, the *DSM-IV-TR* is not without criticism.

One criticism is that the *DSM-IV-TR* was constructed by expert opinion and group consensus. Therefore, while references to source documents are available, the objectivity of the *DSM-IV-TR* is not absolute. As much as it is a product of science, it is a product of idiosyncrasy, social mores, and politics. For example, according to previous versions of the *DSM*, homosexuality was a psychiatric illness, a disease.

Another criticism is that the *DSM-IV-TR* is limited to 297 diagnoses. Indeed, the *DSM-IV-TR* makes little mention of pessimism. In fact, as distressing and destructive as it may be, pessimism is not a mental illness in and of itself. Rather, it is an inclusion criterion for other conditions – that is: depressive personality disorder, mixed anxiety-depressive disorder, and dysthymic disorder – as long as it "cause[s] clinically significant distress or impairment in social, occupational, or other important areas of functioning".

This is perhaps the greatest barrier to rigorous scientific analyses of optimism and pessimism – quite simply: there is no single, widely-accepted means of diagnosing optimism or pessimism. There is no manual. Therefore, several psychological batteries – each with its own strengths and weaknesses – have been constructed in an attempt to define and measure optimism and pessimism. These include: the Hopelessness Scale, the Generalized Expectancy of Success Scale, the Life-Orientation Test, the Optimism-Pessimism Scale, the Future Events Scale, and the Hope Scale.

In 1974, Beck *et al* published the Hopelessness Scale.[2] The authors interviewed clinically-depressed patients who had attempted suicide. They screened the transcriptions and used them to construct a psychological battery comprised of 11 positively-trended and 9 negatively-trended items. Not surprisingly, some of the items were rather grim: "I might as well give up because I can't make things better for myself", "My future seems dark to me", and "I don't expect to get what I really want". Responses were binary; subjects either agreed or disagreed with each item. A tally was obtained and a measure of hopelessness was achieved. Though further study in normal – *id est:* non-suicidal – subject populations demonstrated that the Scale had respectable reliability and validity, its use was largely frowned upon.

Another early test was constructed by Fibel and Hale.[3] The Generalized Expectancy of Success Scale – the GESS – presented subjects with a variety of scenarios. Subjects were asked to evaluate these and to predict likelihoods of success or failure. A measure of expectancies, the Scale began each item with: "In the future, I expect that I will". Responses ranged from "highly improbable" to "highly probable". Fourteen years after its original publication, the GESS was revised in an effort to make it more succinct and more focused. [4] Nevertheless, other psychological batteries had largely supplanted the GESS.

In the mid-1980s, MF Scheier and CS Carver sought "to provide a psychometrically sound measure of optimism, defined in terms of the favorability of a person's generalized outcome expectancy".[5] They continued: "The primary purpose of this article is to report our attempt to begin the exploration of the possibility that optimism, construed as a stable personality characteristic, has important implications for the manner in which people regulate their actions. We propose that optimism may have a variety of consequences, including some that are clearly health-related". With these imperatives, they constructed the Life Orientation Test, the LOT, a questionnaire consisting of 4 positively-oriented, 4 negatively-oriented, and 4 neutral items. An example of a positive item was: "In uncertain times, I usually expect the best"; an example of a negative item was: "If something can go wrong for me, it will". Subjects agreed or disagreed with these items on a multipoint scale and a measure of optimism-pessimism was determined.

In their original research, Scheier and Carver asked their subjects to complete a survey of common physical complaints, including dizziness, blurred vision, muscle soreness, fatigue, *etc*. In an effort to demonstrate that "optimism may have a variety of consequences, including some that are clearly health-related", Scheier and Carver compared their data from the LOT with their data from the health survey. Their results were perhaps not surprising. They concluded that optimists were better able to cope with stress than pessimists. Also, they were less likely to experience – or: at least, report – ill health than pessimists.

The LOT was not without criticism. It was argued that some of the items did not clearly and unequivocally measure an individual subject's expectations of good or bad outcomes – for example: "I always look on the bright side of things" and "I'm a believer in the idea that 'every cloud has a silver lining'" were neither clearly optimistic nor clearly pessimistic. Also, it was argued that the positive and negative items were not related to one another, and, therefore, measured different scales. Indeed, some psychologists have argued that some of the negatively-trended items were better at measuring neuroticism (a persistent negative emotional state characterized by anger, anxiety, confusion, depression, irritability, low sense of self-worth) than they were at measuring pessimism. TW Smith et al wrote: "Thus, the LOT is virtually indistinguishable from measures of neuroticism, and previously reported findings using this scale are perhaps more parsimoniously interpreted as reflecting neuroticism rather than optimism".[6]

In response, Scheier, Carver, and Bridges revised the LOT in 1994 and published the Life Orientation Test – Revised, the LOT-R.[7] Perhaps because of its reliability and validity – or perhaps because of its ease-of-use – the LOT-R became and remains the most popular measure of optimism-pessimism.

A fourth battery is the Optimism-Pessimism Scale, the OPS.[8] Constructed by Dember and associates, it was considerably lengthier and more complicated than the Hopelessness Scale, GESS, LOT, or LOT-R. It included 18 positively-trended items, 18 negatively-trended items, and 20 fillers. Moreover, the OPS, unlike the GESS and the LOT, necessarily treated optimism and pessimism as discrete entities, not as ends of a spectrum; in other words, not as a single bipolar range, but as dual unipolar ranges. Perhaps for this reason, some have suggested that compared to the other psychological instruments, the OPS was more complicated and cumbersome.[9]

While not one and the same, hopefulness and optimism – and hopelessness and pessimism – are certainly interrelated. CR Snyder et al separated hope into two components: 'the will' and 'the ways', or more technically: 'agency' and 'pathways'.[10] They stated: agency "refers to a sense of successful determination in meeting goals in the past, present, and future"; and pathways "refers to a sense of being able to generate successful plans to meet goals". In other words, hope was a union of two beliefs: 1) the attainment of goals is possible, and 2) there are means of attaining those goals. Working within this framework, Snyder et al established the Hope Scale. It included 4 items that determined agency, 4 items that determined pathways, and 4 fillers – for example, agency: "I energetically pursue my goals", and pathways: "I can think of many ways to get out of a jam".

For the Hopelessness Scale, GESS, LOT, OPS, and Hope Scale, each subject provided a discreet –often-numerical – response, a grade. The Attributional Style and Explanatory Style employed a different strategy. These techniques presented subjects with positive or negative outcomes. Then, subjects provided narratives that explained or rationalized the causes of these outcomes. Analyses of these narratives determined whether a subject was optimistic or pessimistic. For example, a subject may have been asked to explain a failing grade on an examination. On one hand, the optimist may have contended that he or she did not study the correct material, did not have enough rest or sleep beforehand, or that the test was simply unfair. On the other hand, the pessimist may have contended that he or she was stupid; in fact, the pessimist may have contended that he or she was doomed to fail any and all tests. By scoring these responses – these descriptions of Attributes and Explanations –, the psychological clinician or researcher determined a subject's measure of optimism-pessimism.[11]

C Peterson *et al* developed a rather interesting variation on the Attributional Style and Explanatory Style, the Content Analysis of Verbal Explanations – the CAVE.[12] This unique approach involved gathering and evaluating numerous written or spoken sources from an individual – *oeuvre*, correspondences, journals, speeches, interviews, *etc*. It searched for explanations of personal events and used these sources to determine the optimistic or pessimistic tendencies of the subjects-in-question. Because it relied on historic data, direct interaction between the psychologist and the subject was not necessary. Therefore, the CAVE technique could be used to determine measures of optimism and pessimism for the deceased, distant, elusive, or fictional patient or subject.

II: WHAT IS THE RELATIONSHIP BETWEEN OPTIMISM AND PESSIMISM?

As hinted above – particularly in the discussion of the Optimism-Pessimism Scale, there was and is a fair degree of controversy in the field of psychology as to the relationship between optimism and pessimism. Psychiatrists and psychologists did not fully appreciate the complexities of optimism-pessimism until the 1970s when the various batteries, including the OPS and LOT, started to evolve. Questions arose: What is the relationship between optimism and pessimism?; Are they two ends of a continuous spectrum – a bipolar continuum?; Or: Are they ends of two separate entities – dual unipolar scales?

Perhaps the best means of illustrating this is with examples from the LOT-R. Again, an example of a positively-trended item is: "In uncertain times, I usually expect the best". Subjects are asked to grade their levels of agreement with this statement in the following way – 0: strongly disagree, 1: disagree, 2: neutral, 3: agree, and 4: strongly agree. Negatively-trended items are reverse scored. Because the LOT-R includes 6 items (3 positive and 3 negative), in theory, scores range from 0 to 24. If viewed as a bipolar continuum, on this scale, optimists have high scores and pessimists have low scores.

However, agreement with a positive item does not necessarily indicate the absence of negativity, nor does disagreement with a positive item necessarily indicate the presence of negativity. Indeed, for the item: "In uncertain times, I usually expect the best", subjects who strongly disagree are not necessarily pessimists; they are non-optimists. Likewise, subjects who strongly disagree with the item: "If something can go wrong for me, it will" are not necessarily optimists; they are non-pessimists. In this model, rather than one range of possible scores from 0 to 24, perhaps two ranges of possible scores from 0 to 12 – one for optimism and one for pessimism – is more fitting.

Insofar as the separation of optimism and pessimism is concerned, the work of PY Herzberg *et al* deserves particular mention.[13] They conducted an extensive analysis of the LOT-R and optimism-pessimism using a large population and rather sophisticated means of controlling biases and confirming psychometrics. Their study population included 46,133 subjects − men and women who ranged in age from 18 to 103 years. This heterogeneous population differed starkly from those of Scheier, Carver, and Bridges, whose study populations consist of a few hundred undergraduate students. In short, Herzberg *et al* found that "the optimism and pessimism items on the LOT–R measure two independent constructs rather than a single, bipolar, continuous trait". Moreover, "the findings were stable across gender, age groups, and groups of medical patients with various diagnoses, and the independence of optimism and pessimism was supported by differential concurrent validity".

Herzberg *et al* argued that the separation of optimism and pessimism was not merely an academic exercise, a theoretical construct without any utility for understanding the human mind. Rather, they stated that it offered insights into what were adaptive, effective, and normal behaviors and coping strategies, and into what were not. "People might, for example, believe that having a certain degree of optimism is adaptive, but they might also believe that having a certain amount of pessimism is also adaptive (e.g., because being pessimistic about the future might help prevent disappointments). These metacognitive beliefs might influence how respondents answer a questionnaire such as the LOT–R." Indeed, Herzberg *et al* noted that this separation of optimism and pessimism was particularly true for older subjects. They argued that this may have been, in fact, a product of the accumulation of life experiences, that this may have represented the continuing maturation of the human mind − *id est:* as one aged, one learned to balance optimism and pessimism.

These differences between optimism and pessimism, and younger and older were perhaps best demonstrated by the works of DK. Mroczek *et al*[14] and S Robinson-Whelen *et al*.[15]

Mroczek *et al* used data from the Normative Aging Study − a large, longitudinal evaluation of men started in 1963 by the Department of Veterans Affairs. Men in the Normative Aging Study had a median age of 60. In other words, they were seniors, the very population that Herzberg *et al* concluded had had the greatest discordance of optimism and pessimism. Mroczek *et al* drew three primary conclusions. First, the LOT conflated optimism with extraversion and pessimism with neuroticism. Second, optimism and pessimism correlated poorly. Third, even when extraversion and neuroticism were controlled, optimism and pessimism were poorly correlated. The first finding was in accord with the work of Smith *et al* – the LOT is not perfect. The second finding was in accord with the work of Herzberg *et al* – optimism and pessimism are distinct entities. Mroczek *et al* found that low optimism and high pessimism correlated with self-reports of mental and physical illness respectively. Also, while low optimism was associated with frequent hassles in life, pessimism was not.

The work of Robinson-Whelen *et al* is most intriguing. Its study population consisted of 224 middle-aged and older adults. Approximately half of this group engaged in the care and management of loved-ones, usually spouses or parents, with chronic illness – for example: Alzheimer's Disease. (Robinson-Whelan *et al* recruited many of their subjects from diagnostic clinics, neurologists' referrals, support groups, and an Alzheimer's-Disease association's newsletters.) Like Herzberg *et al*, Robinson-Whelen *et al* concluded that optimism and pessimism fitted a double-factor model better than a single-factor model. In fact, they argued that the two correlated only weakly with one another in their study population. However, they contended that among individuals experiencing stressors – *id est:* caregivers – non-optimism strongly correlated with pessimism, and *vice versa*. They concluded: "These differences suggest that optimism may not be as pure and independent a measure of positive expectations about the future among stressed individuals. Individuals experiencing an extreme life stressor appear to be less able to perceive that both good and bad things can be expected for the future". Not only did stressed individuals expect the worst, they also reverted to a reality of extremes, one in which only absolute optimism or absolute pessimism was possible – that is: a reality in which the separation of optimism and pessimism disappeared.

Additionally, Robinson-Whelen *et al* sought to determine whether optimism or pessimism could predict a subject's future mental and physical health. They concluded that whereas optimism was unable to so, pessimism was a marker for declining psychological and physiological well-being for both non-stressed and stressed populations. Rather provocatively, Robin-Whelen *et al* titled their work: "Distinguishing optimism from pessimism in older adults: is it more important to be optimistic or not to be pessimistic?" The answer seemed clear: the latter was the case. Not only did pessimists expect the worst, but the worst actually did happen.

Most of the work that used physical-health data to separate optimism and pessimism (including the work described above) did so with self-reported symptoms – for example: self-reported levels of headache, abdominal distress, muscular pain, *etc.* The works of K Räikkönen and KA Matthews, however, did not; they used ambulatory blood pressures. In 2008, they studied the relationship between optimism-pessimism and ambulatory blood pressures in adolescents. [16]

In this report, they followed a cohort of 217 healthy adolescents with ages ranging from 14 to 16 years for a period of two days. Optimism and pessimism scores were obtained using the LOT-R. Räikkönen and Matthews found that blood pressures did not correlate with high or low levels of optimism. However, bloods pressures tended to be higher for subjects with high levels of pessimism compared to subjects with low levels of pessimism. This was true whether the subject was male or female, black or white, fat or thin; whether the blood pressure measured was systolic or diastolic; whether it was day or night.

Moreover, Räikkönen and Matthews compared quartiles of pessimism. The least pessimistic quartile of subjects had blood pressures that were substantially lower than the other three quartiles. In fact, for the latter three quartiles, blood pressures were elevated and not particularly different from one another. Therefore, they drew the following conclusions: first, optimism and pessimism were distinct constructs; and second, the physiological effects of pessimism became manifest after a particular threshold was reached – *id est:* the relationship between pessimism and ambulatory blood pressures was neither linear nor curvilinear. The medical implications of this research – particularly as it related to cardiovascular and end-organ diseases – need not have been stated.

Chapter 3

III: WHAT IS THE RELATIONSHIP BETWEEN OPTIMISM-PESSIMISM AND HEALTH?

A discussion of pessimism and health constitutes the bulk of the present work. As described above, Scheier and Carver's work on the LOT offered a glimpse into some of the early research on optimism-pessimism and physical health. Indeed, this was their original intent: "We propose that optimism may have a variety of consequences, including some that are clearly health-related". In summary: Scheier and Carver asked their subjects to complete a survey of physical complaints, including dizziness, blurred vision, muscle soreness, fatigue, *etc.* They determined that: compared to pessimists, optimists were less likely to report ill health.

Like Scheier and Carver, AS Robbins and colleagues studied optimism-pessimism and health in a population of undergraduate students. Rather provocatively, they titled their work: *Psychological determinants of health and performance: the tangled web of desirable and undesirable characteristics*[17]. In addition to mental and physical health, Robbins *et al* also examined students' health maintenance behaviors and their anticipated and actual academic performances (students' expected course and overall grades, actual course and overall grades, and scores on a nation-wide standardized exam, the Scholastic Aptitude Test or SAT). Robbins *et al*'s results differed somewhat from those of Scheier and Carver. First, *health:* Robbins *et al* found that there was no conclusive and direct link between optimism-pessimism and physical health. Rather, a constellation of negative health characteristics – low self-esteem, pervasive dissatisfaction, a cadre of negative mood states (irritability, anger, guilt, disgust, *etc.*), anxiety, and depression – predicted health complaints. Most interestingly, Robbins *et al* found that a sense of alienation was strongly associated with a sense of poor health in men, but not in women. Second, *academics:* Robbins *et al* found that "achievement strivings made an independent contribution in both sexes to the 2 measures of academic performance". Indeed, they found that a Type-A personality was strongly related to expected and actual academic successes.

Some of the most controversial work on optimism-pessimism and heath came from T Maruta *et al* and C Peterson *et al*. T Maruta *et al* researched the long-term effects of optimism-pessimism on physical health.[18,19] They followed a consecutive series of patients who presented to an Internal-Medical Service for general care between 1962 and 1965, n=1145. Each patient completed the Minnesota Multiphasic Personality Inventory (MMPI). In 1994, Maruta *et al* reevaluated their patients and divided them into two subsets. They included all patients who completed the MMPI, who were from Olmsted County (where the Mayo Clinic was located), and who continued to follow-up with the Mayo Clinic for medical care. Eight-hundred thirty-nine patients – some alive, some deceased – were included by these criteria and were included in the first subset. Maruta *et al* used this population to evaluate the relationship between optimism-pessimism and mortality over a 30-year period. For the second subset, Maruta *et al* included all patients from among the 839 who were still alive. These 447 were asked to complete the Short-Form Health Survey (SF-36), a review of 36 common physical health complaints. They used these data to determine the long-term effects of optimism-pessimism on mental and physical health over a 30-year period.

First: *Mortality.* Over the course of 30-years, optimists were more likely to survive than pessimists. This was true even when age and gender were controlled. Indeed, on multivariate modeling, "mortality increased 19% for every 10-point T-score increase". This study was not designed to provide an explanation for this intriguing finding. Nonetheless, Maruta *et al* posited that optimism may have protected subjects from depression and learned helplessness; that optimism may have promoted seeking and receiving medical help; that it may have protected against self-blame and catastrophic thinking; or that it may have modulated the immune system, protecting against inflammatory threats.

Second: *Health.* In short, Maruta *et al* found that optimists fared better than pessimists in terms of mental and physical health. "More specifically, an optimistic explanatory style is associated with a self-report of fewer limitations due to health; fewer problems with work or other daily activities as a result of physical health; less pain and fewer limitations due to pain and, conversely, better personal health; feeling more energetic most of the time; performing social activities with less interference from physical or emotional problems; fewer problems with work or other daily activities as a result of emotional state; and feeling more peaceful, happier, and calmer most of the time". Pessimism was associated with poorer health in each and every health domain of the SF-36.

While the works of Maruta *et al* included large numbers of subjects, it relied upon self-reported data. Peterson *et al* mitigated this subjectivity by using subjects from the Study of Adult Development at the Harvard University Health Sciences, a longitudinal investigation started in 1937 to study "the kinds of people who are well and do well".[20] Undergraduate students enrolled at Harvard College were screened for academic success, and mental and physical health. Upon study entry, they completed a battery of personality and intelligence tests. After graduation, they completed annual surveys on employment, family, health, and general well-being. Moreover, data were obtained from each subject's primary-care physician. The study continued over a course of 35 years.

Peterson *et al* determined that optimism-pessimism did not influence the health of their subjects immediately – *id est*: at study entry. However, around the ages of 35 to 50 years, the interrelationship between optimism-pessimism and health became apparent. "Pessimistic explanatory style (the belief that bad events are caused by stable, global, and internal factors) predicted poor health at ages 45-60, even when physical and mental health at age 25 were controlled. Pessimism in early adulthood appears to be a risk factor for poor health in middle and late adulthood." According to the authors, the correlations between optimism and good health, and pessimism and poor health was strongest at 45 years of age.

These studies – by Maruta *et al* and Peterson *et al* –, drew rather definitive conclusions: over a period of several decades, optimism was associated with good mental and physical health, and pessimism was associated with poor health. Other studies – particularly those by Achat *et al* – have provided variations on these results. Achat *et al* studied 659 subjects in the Normative Aging Study – as mentioned earlier, a large, prospective study of healthy middle-aged and older men followed by the Veterans Administration.[21] They utilized the LOT, the Center for Epidemiologic Studies – Depression Scale, and the Medical Outcomes Study Short-Form Health Survey. The authors found: "optimism was associated with higher levels of general health perceptions, vitality, and mental health, and lower levels of bodily pain". Two smaller studies by Achat *et al* – which included both men and women – found similar findings.[22,23] Moreover, the authors found that compared to pessimism, optimists were more likely to refrain from smoking, to moderate alcohol intake, and to engage in brisk walking and other vigorous activities. In other words, "dispositional optimism is associated with healthy aging"; optimists grew older both energetically and gracefully.

Most studies relied upon self-reports of health, leaving the possibility of disconnects between perceived and actual states of health. Indeed, one may be optimistic but moribund, or pessimistic and robust. Ruthing *et al*, in a large study of 8305 middle-aged and elderly Native Americans – with a mean age of 68.36 years –, attempted to address this.[24] The authors collected both subjective and objective measures of health. By comparing these to one another, the authors established a measure of congruence – realists were those whose subjective and objective health was similar; optimists believed their health was better than it actually was; and pessimists believed that their health was worse than it actually was. Moreover, the authors examined each subject's functional well-being, social well-being, and hospital admissions.

Most subjects (65%) were fairly realistic about their health – 37% of subjects were aware of their good health; and 28% of subjects were aware of their poor health. Twenty percent were optimists and overestimated their health; and 15% were pessimists and underestimated their health. These findings offered intriguing insights. First, most people demonstrated fairly accurate interpretations of their health. Second, optimism was more common than pessimism. Also, perhaps not surprisingly, compared to optimists, pessimists were less likely to be independent in their activities of daily living (ADLs), to exercise, to be socially engaged, and more likely to be hospitalized. Indeed, herein a paradoxical finding – indeed, a finding with profound public-health implications – became evident: the pessimist, even one at the peak of health, was more likely than the optimist with extreme physical debilitation to present to the clinic, ward, or nursing home.

As evident, the majority of the studies outlined above dealt with optimism in and of itself or as part of the optimism-pessimism axis. Though most studies made note of pessimism, particularly as an element of depression, few directly addressed pessimism as an element of its own. One study that separated optimism and pessimism was conducted by A Scioli and colleagues at Keene State College in New Hampshire.[25] This group studied the relationships between optimism-pessimism, hopefulness-hopelessness, and physical health in a group of 57 undergraduate students enrolled in an introductory-psychology course. In an attempt to limit the influence of confounding variables – particularly in light of a small subject population –, this study incorporated several controls. For example: in their analysis of pessimism and health, they controlled for neuroticism, depression, and alienation.

As perhaps expected, Scioli and colleagues found that optimistic and hopeful individuals were more likely to experience better health over a ten-week period, and pessimistic and hopeless individuals were more likely to experience worse health over a ten-week period. However, when they controlled for neuroticism, correlations between pessimism and ill-health became non-significant. Correlations between hopelessness and ill-health, on the other hand, stayed significant. In fact, the authors reported that "only 16% of the variance in hope scores was explained by the variation in optimism scores". Therefore, though small, this study demonstrated 1) optimism-pessimism and hopefulness-hopelessness were indeed different entities; and 2) optimism and pessimism were not two ends of a continuum, but rather two separate entities.

Scioli *et al*'s work begged the question: what were the differences between optimism and hopefulness? While they posited several intriguing possibilities, they did not draw any definitive conclusions. One theory was that optimism mediated minor life hassles, day-to-day annoyances, whereas hopefulness mediated major life disasters, profound threats to individual well-being, including diseases and injuries. Therefore, compared to the hopeful person, the optimistic person was less capable of coping with significant stresses. In the long run, hope was more beneficial than optimism.

A sense of personal control was another important component of the interrelationships between optimism-pessimism, hopefulness-hopelessness, and health. While they did not draw any specific conclusions, they recognized that surely interrelationships existed. Perhaps it was a sense of personal control that allowed the optimist and hopeful individual to thrive. And correspondingly, perhaps it was an absence of a sense of personal control that allowed the pessimist and hopeless individual to fail. Indeed, this seemed much in line with the work of Synder *et al* who argued that hope was an amalgamation of 'the wills' and 'the ways', of agency and pathway. The hopeful individual, who expected good outcomes and who felt a sense of personal control in the attainment of those outcomes, had better health outcomes. The hopeless individual, who expected poor outcomes and who did not feel a sense of personal control, had worse health outcomes.

This finding was supported in a small study of senior citizens living in Canada.[26] Ruthing *et al* studied the role of personal control and optimism-pessimism in determining individual mental and physical well-being. More specifically, they examined senior citizens' perceptions of their personal risks of suffering and surviving hip fractures, and the degrees of personal control and optimism-pessimism they expressed. For those who felt a strong sense of personal control, optimism predicted improved well-being compared to pessimism. For those who did not feel a strong sense of personal control, there was no relationship between optimism-pessimism and well-being. This finding seemed to suggest that a strong sense of personal control was necessary for the mental and physical health outcomes of optimism and pessimism to become manifest.

Umstattd *et al*, in a study of senior citizens, achieved similar results.[27] They used several objective measures for physical functioning, including the speed and deftness with which subjects walked a specified distance and climbed a specified number of stairs. On initial analysis, the authors found: pessimism and a low sense of self-efficacy corresponded to poor physical functioning. However, when controlling for a low sense of self-efficacy, the relationship between pessimism and poor physical functioning was attenuated. Umstattd *et al* found no relationship between optimism and physical functioning. Therefore, they concluded that optimism and pessimism played no role in determining physical functioning, that it was a sense of self-efficacy that determined physical functioning. Again, these findings seemed to suggest: perhaps it was not disposition in and of itself, but rather the combination of disposition and agency that directed health, function, and well-being.

These three works – by Scioli *et al*, Ruthig *et al*, and Umstattd *et al* – demonstrated the complex interplay between optimism-pessimism, hopefulness-hopelessness, control-helplessness, efficacy-inefficacy, and mental and physical health, an interplay that extends beyond the premise: optimism is good and pessimism is bad. And in doing so, they added to the works of Maruta *et al* and Peterson *et al*; they provided intricacies and nuances. However, this also opened the door for further discord among various authors and their works. For example: Scioli demonstrated a relationship between optimism and good health; Ruthig demonstrated that this relationship existed only when the individual felt a strong sense of personal control; Umstattd demonstrated that optimism and physical function were not related at all. Scioli, Ruthig, and Umstattd went deeper into the psychology of pessimism than Maruta and Peterson – but, by going deeper, they arrived at different positions.

Also, certainly, there could also have been mundane explanations for these discordant findings. Some of these discordances were attributable to the differences between the study populations – men versus women, old versus young, students versus retirees, etc. And some of these were attributable to the differences in the techniques used in measuring mental and physical health. Finally, some of these were attributable to the fact that the breadth of human experience was and is broad; that the interplay between mind and body is complicated; that, as of yet, psychiatric and psychological evaluations of optimism-pessimism and mental and physical health are neither perfect nor conclusive. Certainly, further study is required.

PESSIMISM AND HEATH HABITS

The works of Achat *et al* were discussed above. In summary, they found that compared to their pessimistic counterparts, optimistic senior citizens were more likely to engage in healthy lifestyles: to refrain from smoking, to moderate alcohol consumption, to engage in physical activity. Smaller studies found similar findings in different patient populations.

Carvajal *et al*[28] and Taylor *et al* [29]studied the relationship between optimism-pessimism and health habits in children. The former found that in a group of 525 boys and girls with a mean age of 12.3 years, those with higher positive global expectancies – higher levels of optimism and hopefulness – were less likely to use alcohol, cigarettes, and marijuana. The latter used data from the Girls' Health Enrichment Multisite Studies, a multicenter research initiative aimed at investigating and preventing childhood obesity. Ninety-two Afro-American girls, who ranged in age from 8 to 10 years, were randomized into two groups. One group engaged in intense dietary and physical therapies; the other group served as a matched control. Both groups completed numerous psychological batteries, including the Youth-LOT. Taylor *et al* found that optimists were more likely to increase their levels of physical activity. However, they were also more likely to consume a greater percentage of calories from fats. The authors did not provide an explanation for this seemingly counterproductive pair of trends.

Kelloniemi *et al* conducted a somewhat similar study.[30] In 1966, 11,637 people were born in Northern Finland and enrolled into a national database. From among these, 8,690 subjects completed questionnaires evaluating their demographics, their degree of optimism-pessimism, and their health habits. Overall, optimists had better health habits than pessimists. While both were as likely to consume junk food, optimists were more likely than pessimists to consume foods high in fiber and low in fat. Indeed, "the proportion of pessimistic subjects who ate sausages daily and healthy foods infrequently was higher than that of optimistic subjects". Also, compared to pessimists, optimists were also less likely to be obese – this was particularly true among women. Finally, compared to pessimists, optimists were less likely to drink alcohol, smoke tobacco, and consume caffeinated beverages.

However, another study arrived at different results.[31] KR Fontaine and LJ Cheskin, who followed 177 adult patients enrolled in a clinic-based based weight loss program, found that optimism-pessimism was not associated with degree of weight loss or with compliance with program guidelines. However, compared to optimists, pessimists tended to remained enrolled in the weight loss program longer. "Perhaps this association reflects that pessimists, who characteristically do not expect the best, are not very confident in their personal resources or prospects of success and thereby rely heavily on the weight loss program itself". In other words, unable to rely on themselves, pessimists learned to rely on others – but overall, both optimists and pessimists had unhealthy diets and engaged in minimal exercise.

Despite this dependence upon others – particularly members of the healthcare community –, compared to optimists, pessimists seemed to develop a rather paradoxical and profound dislike of those to whom they had turned. Indeed, Costello *et al* performed a study into the relationship between optimism-pessimism and patient satisfaction among 11,636 individuals presenting to an outpatient medical clinic.[32] Overall, subjects seemed to approve of their encounters with their healthcare providers. However, compared to those who scored high on the optimism scale of the Minnesota Multiphasic Personality Inventory, those who scored high on the pessimism scale were much less likely to be satisfied. Whereas 72% of optimists rated these encounters as having been excellent, only 59% of pessimists did the same. Surprisingly, these ratings matched those expressed by non-hostile and hostile patients: 66% and 57% respectively. The clinical implications of these findings were and are clear and significant insofar as a mutually supportive physician-patient relationship was and is tantamount to establishing trust, cooperation, compliance, and health-promotion.

A similar conclusion was achieved in a study of 40 family members of critically-ill patients – some with cancer and some without – admitted to an intensive-care unit in the United States.[33] All subjects completed the LOT, the Acute Stress Disorder Scale, the Brief System Inventory, the Critical Care Family Needs Inventory, and the Impact Message Inventory. The authors found that compared to optimists, pessimists were less satisfied with the care provided by critical-care physicians and nurses; they reported less affiliation and more disconnection with the medical staff, and, indeed, reported feeling as though they were 'being controlled'.

PESSIMISM AND DENTAL CARE

A surprisingly sizeable amount of the literature is devoted to the relationship between optimism-pessimism and dental care. Much of this work comes from Scandinavia, where national governments and healthcare systems keep longitudinal data on all residents. Two studies came from Finland.[34,35] Ylöstalo *et al* sent questionnaires to all Finns born in the northern provinces of Lapland and Oulu in 1966. Of 11,541 potential subjects, 8,690 – 75.3% – responded. At the time of the study, all subjects were 31 years of age. The authors found that compared to pessimists, optimists were more likely to report good dental health (less likely to report caries, gingival bleeding, and oral pain); more likely to brush their teeth at least twice per day; more likely to seek checkups; and more likely to avoid sugared beverages.

Reasons for these behaviors – good dental care for optimists; bad dental care for pessimists – were perhaps obvious. Compared to optimists, pessimists were less able to envision and to seek a future of good oral hygiene – they lacked the disposition, hopefulness, control, and efficacy. Moreover, it may very well have been the case that compared to optimists, pessimists simply feared the dentist and dental work more. Indeed, a small study from the United Kingdom demonstrated that both pessimists and optimists overestimated the degree of pain that dental checkups entailed. However, the degree of overestimation was substantially higher for pessimists than for optimists.[36]

PESSIMISM AND NEUROLOGIC DISEASE

Traumatic Brain Injury. T Tomberg *et al* conducted two small studies of patients with traumatic brain injuries.[37,38] In one study, the authors compared 85 patients with traumatic brain injuries with 68 normal controls using various batteries, including the LOT-R and numerous measures of health-related quality of life. They found that compared to controls, patients with traumatic brain injuries were less likely to have and to use social support networks, were less likely to be satisfied with their social support networks, and were less likely to be optimistic. Among subjects with traumatic brain injuries, those individuals who demonstrated apt coping skills, satisfaction with social support networks, and optimistic dispositions were the most likely to express good quality of life and the most likely to return to work after injury. The second study was a follow-up to this. It demonstrated that while patients with traumatic brain injuries reported increasing optimism, this did not correspond to the development or maturation of coping skills, to increasing use of and satisfaction with social support networks, or to increasing rates of employment. Therefore, while dispositions may have improved over time, rehabilitation with continued social and psychological support mechanisms was required for this population.

Epilepsy. The unpredictability of seizures may hinder an epileptic patient's ability to establish a self of personal control and his or her ability to function socially – to work, to establish friendships, to drive an automobile. Moreover, increasing frequencies and severities of seizures of may correspond to increasing rates of pessimism, hopelessness, helplessness, and depression.[39] According to one study, patients with epilepsy "are easily hurt, and they often fear that others try to take advantage of them. Accordingly, they have a tendency to keep problems and reactions to themselves, and an effort is needed to establish a good relationship with them".[40] In other words, epileptics demonstrated learned helplessness; in general, their outlooks for the future were bleak.

Multiple Sclerosis. Multiple sclerosis – a chronic disease in which immune cells attack the central nervous system, thereby causing anatomic and functional neurological lesions – is associated with persistent pessimism and depression. [41] For these patients, intensive multidisciplinary rehabilitation may improve qualities of life – decreasing the prevalence of disabilities and pessimistic dispositions.[42]

Parkinson's Disease. Depression is common among those with Parkinson's Disease, affecting somewhere between 22.6 to 53.6% of patients.[43] The most reliable indicators of depression in this population are: dysphoria, irritability, sadness, suicidal ideation, and pessimism. Selective serotonin reuptake inhibitors have been shown to be beneficial for these patients.

One study – by Lyons *et al* – evaluated the relationship between optimism-pessimism and health in 311 male and female caregivers of patients with Parkinson's Disease.[44] All subjects completed the LOT and surveys of physical and psychological health. The authors followed this population for 10 years. Compared to optimists, pessimists exhibited worse physical and psychological health at baseline and a faster decline in health over the course of the study.

Facial Pain. A few studies investigating the relationship between optimism-pessimism and facial pain have been conducted. One study – one that evaluated facial pain in a population that included all 5,696 men and women born in Northern Finland in 1966 – used the LOT-R and concluded: compared to optimists, pessimists were more likely to report facial pain.[45] Another – rather complicated – study, conducted among 20 subjects with and 28 subjects without temporal-mandibular pain, examined the relationships between optimism-pessimism, stress, temporal-mandibular pain, and serum levels of epinephrine, norepinephrine, and interleukin-6. During stressful situations, control subjects displayed statistically significant increases in levels of serum norepinephrine and interleukin-6. Study subjects did not display these increases; the responses of interleukin-6 were particularly blunted. Moreover, among the control subjects, optimists and pessimists demonstrated similar levels of norepinephrine and interleukin-6. However, among the study subjects, compared to optimists, pessimists displayed higher levels of these biochemicals. These data were very complicated and certainly difficult to interpret. Also, their applicability was limited by a somewhat small study population. Nonetheless, one fact was clear and noteworthy: during stressful situations, those with pain and those without pain, and optimists and pessimists expressed different serum levels of norepinephrine and interleukin-6.[46]

Pediatric Neurological Disorders. Some work on optimism-pessimism and psychosocial health has been done in parents of children with neurological disorders. In a study by Lamontagne *et al*, 60 parents of children undergoing spinal surgery completed the LOT, Spielberger's State Anxiety Scale, and Ways of Coping Questionnaire.[47] All subjects were followed from the preoperative to the postoperative period. After surgery, all subjects demonstrated decreased levels of psychological distress. However, overall, compared to optimists, pessimists were less able to cope with stressors. Another study was conducted by Labbee *et al.*[48] They examined a population of 52 caregivers of children with neurological disorders – 32 had Batten's Disease, an inherited, terminal, neuro-degenerative disorder; and 20 had either epilepsy or cerebral palsy, two decidedly less devastating disorders. The results were perhaps not surprising: compared to parents of children with epilepsy or cerebral palsy, parents of children with Batten's Disease exhibited lower degrees of optimism, higher degrees of pessimism, and more psychological distress. Moreover, the authors found a direct relationship between optimism-pessimism and distress – optimists coped well; pessimists coped poorly.

PESSIMISM AND SENSORY IMPAIRMENT

Visual Impairment. Loneliness results from disparities between desired and actual levels of social interactions. Therefore, hindrances to social interactions – including sensory impairments – may give rise to loneliness. Using the LOT-R, CR Barron *et al* argued that "optimism and social support satisfaction were found to predict degree of loneliness... Women who were less optimistic and less satisfied with their social support system experience higher levels of loneliness".[49] In fact, "Optimism, together with social support satisfaction, explained approximately 43% of the variance in degree of loneliness." These interrelationships did not change even when age, marital status, and health were controlled. However, duration of visual impairment did correspond with duration of loneliness – the longer one was visually impaired, the longer one was lonely.

Auditory Impairment. B Scott *et al* from the University of Uppsala in Sweden conducted an intriguing study.[50] They exposed 40 hearing impaired subjects to three stressful scenarios each during which communicational skills were tested. For each subject, the authors determined levels of optimism-pessimism, senses of control, and abilities to cope with and overcome the stressful scenarios at hand. The results were perhaps not surprising: individuals with optimistic dispositions and senses of control fared better than those with pessimistic dispositions and no senses of control.

In regard to those with auditory impairments, the importance of the interrelationship between sense of control and successful communication may be obvious – the hearing impaired individual must be able to feel in control of a stressful scenario so as to direct the course of action towards successful communication. In these situations, those with no sense of control may be quite literally deafened or muted – hindered from social interactions – by their inability to cope with the stress of communicating with people without auditory impairments. Moreover, whereas the optimist believes that good outcomes are possible – even during these stressful situations –, the pessimist does not. Optimists strive to achieve successful communication; pessimists do not.

PESSIMISM AND BLOOD PRESSURE

Some of the research into optimism-pessimism and blood pressure was discussed previously. Again: Räikkönen and Matthews concluded that in a cohort of 217 healthy adolescents with ages ranging from 14 to 16 years, optimism and blood pressure did not correspond; however, pessimism and blood pressure were directly related to one another. Indeed, a mild pessimist tended to have a lower blood pressure than a moderate or severe pessimist. Räikkönen and Matthews conducted a similar study in a population of 100 adult men and women ranging in age from 30 to 45 years.[51] Interestingly, whereas in children, variations in optimism did not correspond to variations in blood pressures, in adults, they did; subjects with high measures of optimism had lower blood pressures, and subjects with low measures of optimism had higher blood pressures. Moreover, when optimistic individuals felt negative, their blood pressures increased to levels similar to those observed in their pessimistic counterparts. As in children, in the adult population, degree of pessimism was directly associated with elevated blood pressures. Despite subtle differences, both studies by Räikkönen and Matthews seemed to suggest that in general, optimists tended to have lower blood pressures and pessimists tended to have higher blood pressures. The physical health implications of these findings were significant and needed not to have been stated.

Grewen *et al* conducted a small, but thorough, investigation of optimism-pessimism and blood pressure in a group of 37 middle-aged women aged from 39-64 years.[52] All women were postmenopausal, not on hormone-replacement therapy, and not on antihypertensive medication. In addition to measures of optimism-pessimism and ambulatory blood pressures, the authors also collected demographic data, as well as data on catecholamines levels in the urine – epinephrine and norepinephrine. While pessimism and low socioeconomic status were not associated with elevated blood pressures independently, in conjunction, they were. Indeed, women who were both pessimistic and from impoverished backgrounds – impoverished pessimists – demonstrated higher systolic and diastolic blood pressures. Interestingly, 57% of these women demonstrated blood pressures within the range of clinical hypertension – systolic blood pressure greater than 140 mm-Hg and diastolic blood pressure greater than 90 mm-Hg. The other three groups – privileged optimists, privileged pessimists, and impoverished optimists – included fewer subjects with hypertensive blood pressures – 8-29%. Moreover, compared to the other groups, impoverished pessimists demonstrated higher concentrations of urinary epinephrine and higher ratios of urinary epinephrine to norepinephrine; there were no differences in the concentrations of urinary norepinephrine. Perhaps these findings were not surprising – pessimists demonstrated difficulty coping with stressful situations; the impoverished encountered stressful situations frequently.

Finally, one report conducted among 1,021 hypertensive male and female Finns investigated rates of compliance and noncompliance with medications among optimists and pessimists.[53] In total, 60% of subjects were totally compliant, 36% partially compliant, and 4% totally noncompliant. Perhaps unexpectedly, optimism-pessimism was not associated with compliance-noncompliance – optimists were just as likely as pessimists to be compliant or to be noncompliant with their antihypertensive medications. Although the implications of hypertension and although the effects of antihypertensive medications were not particularly apparent in the acute period, both optimists and pessimists seemed to be able to project and accept the long-term benefits of diligence with pharmacological treatment. However, caution must be used in interpreting the results of this study – despite a relatively large size, its subject population was rather homogenous: middle-class Finnish men and women – that is, rather highly educated individuals with open and free access to healthcare and medications.

PESSIMISM AND CARDIAC AND VASCULAR DISEASE

There has been much work on the relationship between psychosocial factors and cardiac and vascular disease. The INTERHEART Study – a multinational evaluation of stress and cardiac disease in 11,119 patients – was particularly noteworthy for its scope. It found that stress in general, stress at home, stress at work, financial stress, and depression were risk factors for cardiovascular disease.[54] One recent meta-analysis concluded: "based on prospective epidemiological data, there was evidence for an association between depression, social support, and psychological work characteristics and coronary heart disease aetiology and prognosis".[55,56]

Unfortunately, while the literature on psychological characteristics and cardiac and vascular disease is broad, most of it focuses on stress, personality, and depression. Studies assessing optimism-pessimism and cardiac and vascular disease directly are comparatively sparse. Some of this work evaluated optimism-pessimism as a predictor of risk; some as a predictor of long-term recovery; and some as a predictor of perioperative complications. Each is discussed below.

Cardiac and Vascular Disease Risk. Some of the most thorough work on the relationship between optimism-pessimism and cardiac and vascular disease was conducted by Kubzansky *et al*. Intriguingly, they titled one of their works: *Is the glass half empty or half full? A prospective study of optimism and coronary heart disease in the Normative Aging Study.*[57] They used data from the Normative Aging Study, which, as previously described, was a large, prospective, multifaceted evaluation of subjects followed by the Veterans Administration of the United States. The authors used the Optimism-Pessimism Scale to determine each subject's degrees of optimism and pessimism. Over an average of 10 years of follow-up, from amongst a cohort of 1,306 subjects, there were 162 cardiac events. Of these, 102 were cases of myocardial infarction – 71 nonfatal, and 31 fatal. For the most part, these phenomena were less common amongst optimists and more common amongst pessimists. On multivariate analysis, compared to men with high measures of pessimism, men with high measures of optimism demonstrated a relative risk reduction of 0.44 (with a 95% confidence interval of 0.26-0.74) for myocardial infarction, and a relative risk reduction of 0.45 (with a 95% confidence interval of 0.29-0.68) for all cardiac events. Moreover, there was a dose-response relationship between optimism and cardiac event risk reduction – the greater the optimist, the greater the reduction in cardiac event risk. Kubzansky *et al* concluded: "These results suggest that an optimistic explanatory style may protect against risk of coronary heart disease in older men". Later studies arrived at similar findings.[58,59]

While these studies posited several possibilities, they did not offer any definite explanations for their findings. It was certainly plausible that optimists were better at adjusting to stressful situations – for example: a new diagnosis of hypertension, an acute myocardial infarction, or a stroke – and were, therefore, better at projecting and pursuing positive futures. Quite simply, they coped better. However, a growing body of evidence suggested that these phenomena had physiological origins, that there were biological explanations for the health benefits of optimism and the health detriments of pessimism. Two compelling studies – one by Everson et al. [60] and one by Matthews et al. [61]– examined the relationships between optimism-pessimism and carotid artery atherosclerosis. The former used data from The Kuopio Ischemic Heart Disease Risk Factor Study, a longitudinal study conducted in Kuopio, Finland – a region with high rates of cardiac morbidity and mortality. Ultimately, a total of 1,038 middle-aged men were enrolled. Each subject completed the Hopelessness Scale and underwent two bilateral carotid Duplexes – one at baseline and one at an average of 4 years afterwards. Comparisons of these ultrasounds provided an objective measure of the progression of atherosclerotic disease. Overall, compared to men with low measures of hopelessness, men with high measures of hopelessness had a 19.2% increase in maximal intimal-medial thickness, a 21.8% increase in mean intimal-medial thickness, and a 10.0% increase in plaque height. Moreover, these findings were most pronounced in subjects who reported persistent, unrelenting levels of hopelessness. Interestingly, the relationship between hopelessness and the progression of atherosclerotic disease was only evident in subjects who had had moderate or severe disease at baseline.

The work of Matthews et al differed only slightly – Everson and colleagues assessed hopefulness-hopelessness using the Hopelessness Scale; Matthews and colleagues assessed optimism-pessimism using the LOT; the former studied middle-aged Finnish men; the latter, middle-aged American women; the former used 4-year follow-up carotid ultrasounds; the latter, 3-year. Overall, the two studies arrived at rather similar conclusions. Matthews et al demonstrated that while optimists and pessimists did not differ in maximum or mean intimal-medial thickness at study entry, they demonstrate different rates of disease progression over the course of 3-years of follow-up. In other words, whereas optimists showed virtually no evidence of worsening atherosclerotic disease, pessimists did. Moreover, the relationship between optimism-pessimism and atherosclerotic progression seemed dose-dependent – the most optimistic quartile demonstrated no disease progression; the other three-quartiles demonstrated similar levels of disease progression. In other words, after a specific threshold of optimism-pessimism was reached, the benefits of optimism and the consequences of pessimism were attenuated.

Matthews and colleagues did not offer an explanation for their findings. However, they did compare this study to some of their other studies, particularly those that examined the relationship between optimism-pessimism and ambulatory blood pressures. Indeed, all of these works concluded that optimism was physiologically beneficial, and that pessimism was physiologically detrimental. Moreover, dose-dependence was observed in both relationships: between optimism-pessimism and carotid atherosclerosis, and optimism-pessimism and blood pressures. Therefore, the authors suggested that: perhaps optimists demonstrated decreased blood pressures and, consequentially, less carotid pathology; and perhaps the obverse was the case for pessimists. Nevertheless, carotid disease and stroke have complicated pathophysiologies – including but extending beyond persistent and progressive hypertension; not all hypertensive patients develop stroke, and not all stroke patients demonstrate hypertension. Therefore, while Matthews, Räikkönen, and colleagues offered an important and intriguing clue into the interplay of mind and body, more experimentation and data were and are necessary.

Fortunately, animal studies have started to fulfill this need, to offer an enticing explanation of the relationship between optimism-pessimism and cardiac and vascular disease.[62] Evidence from research into monkeys suggested that both acute and chronic exposures to psychosocial stressors could cause excessive and persistent activations of the sympathetic nervous system as well as excessive and persistent elevations of serum cortisol levels. In turn, these phenomena could lead to: accelerated atherosclerosis; endothelial and platelet dysfunction; increased hematological viscosity; increased vasoconstriction – *id est:* arterial hypertension and cardiac strain; the generation and promotion of irregular, pathologic – and potentially lethal – heart rhythms; and cardiac ischemia.

Long-term Recovery After Cardiac and Vascular Events. Certainly, myocardial infarctions are stressful emotionally and physically. Several studies have sought to determine the ability of individuals to cope with these stressors. Two studies – one conducted in 1984 and one conducted in 2006 essentially arrived at the same conclusions.

The older study was conducted by Wiklund *et al*; they evaluated a cohort of 177 consecutive Swedish males who had had a myocardial infarction one year prior to study enrollment.[63] All subjects were less than 61 years of age and were fully functional prior to the event. This element was essential to the study insofar as it attempted to evaluate the ability of healthy individuals to achieve recovery to baseline – *id est:* pre-event – function. The authors found that emotional states were relatively stable − optimists at time of myocardial infarction tended to be optimistic two months and twelve months afterwards. Also, compared to a control population, the subject population demonstrated increased emotional distress, avoidant behaviors − particularly in regards to return to work and leisure activities −, overprotection and anxiety, pessimism, physical symptoms, and diminished libido.

Two decades later, a study by Brink *et al* added to these conclusions; they found that in a similar population − 98 Swedish men and women who had suffered a myocardial infarction within a year of enrollment −, optimism-pessimism and fatigue were directly related; optimists reported less fatigue and pessimists reported more fatigue.[64] Therefore, perhaps not surprising, compared to optimists, pessimists were reluctant to engage in work and play, more likely to complain of physical symptoms, and more likely to refrain from sex. Depression and fatigue were not related.

Another Swedish study − The Secondary Prevention in Uppsala Primary Health Care Project (The SUPRIM Study), which evaluated 346 men and women who had suffered myocardial infarction within one year of enrollment − achieved somewhat different results.[65] As in the studies by Wicklund *et al* and Brink *et al*, compared to a control population, the subject population tended to report poorer health, and tended to avoid work and leisure. However, in this study, subject and control populations demonstrated no differences in optimism or pessimism. Indeed, female gender was the only risk factor for decreased optimism and increased pessimism for individuals both with and without a history of cardiac disease.

Peri-operative Complications. According to several studies, compared to optimists, pessimists faired worse after coronary artery bypass grafting. The largest of these studies was conducted by Halpin and Barnett.[66] They evaluated 565 patients undergoing elective coronary artery bypass grafting at a single, large hospital in northern Virginia. After adjusting for age, gender, and disease severity, the authors found that compared to optimists, pessimists required 1.3 days of additional hospitalization, a statistically significant finding. Moreover, compared to optimists, pessimists were more likely to experience prolonged ventilation and permanent stroke; odds ratios were 5.15 with a 95% confidence interval of 1.35-19.64 and 9.56 with a 95% confidence interval of 1.11-82.38 respectively.

This trend seemed to continue throughout the post-operative period. In two studies of men and women undergoing elective coronary artery bypass grafting, Scheier *et al* found that in the first six months after surgery, optimists were more likely to return to work and to resume leisure activities; pessimists were more likely to require repeat hospitalizations.[67,68] Reasons for readmission included:

sternal wound infection, angina, myocardial infarction, and the need for further interventions, including percutaneous coronary intervention and coronary artery bypass grafting. Another study found that two factors predicted the likelihood of chest-wall discomfort in women who underwent coronary artery bypass grafting: use of an internal mammary artery graft and a persistent pessimistic disposition.[69] All relationships between optimism-pessimism and re-hospitalization were independent of subject demographics and psychological and medical histories – including low self-esteem, neuroticism, and depression.

Ben-Zur et al offered psychological explanations for these findings. They noted: "Although the operation was successful for these patients and their functional capacity was improved, it still consisted of a major life-threatening event, with long-term trauma leading to anxiety and other mood changes that are difficult to overcome. Moreover, these patients may have realized their vulnerability for the first time, and the possibility of death may have become more concrete than ever before. [Also], patients might have hope[s] that their level of functioning would be highly improved and their hope[s] were not entirely fulfilled. Such disappointment may underlie their continued anxiety and mood changes, and may lead to uncertainty concerning future heath"[70]. Quite simply: compared to optimists, pessimists could not cope with the burdens of disease; they could not emerge from the depths of illness.

PESSIMISM AND RESPIRATORY DISEASE

Like cardiac and vascular diseases, respiratory diseases are ubiquitous – chronic obstructive pulmonary disease, also known as emphysema or chronic bronchitis, and asthma are two of the most common. However, the relationship between optimism-pessimism and pathologies of the heart and vessels is much more thoroughly investigated than the relationship between optimism-pessimism and pathologies of the airways and lungs. Nonetheless, a handful of insightful and interesting studies exist and warrant attention.

Pulmonary Function. Kubzansky et al used data from the Normative Aging Study to determine the relationship between optimism-pessimism and pulmonary function.[71] Over the course of 8 years of follow-up, the authors found that in a population of 670 middle-aged and senior men registered with the Veterans Administration of the United States, whereas optimists tended to exhibit better pulmonary function, pessimists tended to exhibit worse pulmonary function. Indeed, compared to the latter, the former had fared better on two measures of lung mechanics, the forced expiratory volume in 1 second and the forced vital capacity. Moreover, while these measures declined naturally in all subjects as they aged, they tended to decline less rapidly in optimists and more rapidly in pessimists. These findings were independent of whether the subject did or did not smoke. The theoretical implications of these findings were profound. However, the clinical utility of these findings was limited insofar as it was unknown whether optimism begat better breathing or better breathing begat optimism.

Chronic Obstructive Pulmonary Disease. According to the American Lung Association, individuals with chronic obstructive pulmonary disease [COPD] report that the condition hinders activities of daily life profoundly, limiting the ability to work, engage in physical activities, complete household shores, engage in social and family activities, and sleep.[72] Indeed, some patients with COPD cannot complete tasks without becoming short-of-breath; others cannot live without supplemental oxygen in constant tow – a grim prospect indeed, one capable of setting the psychological foundations of pessimism, hopelessness, and helplessness. However, according one study, this was not necessarily the case. Alberto and Joyner investigated a population of 68 subjects with COPD who attended a community-based support group.[73] Overall, they found that all individuals in this study expressed high degrees of hope, optimism, and self-care. However, compared to individuals with greater measures of hope and optimism, those with lesser measures of hope and optimism demonstrated less self-care. In other words, the authors found that optimism was necessary for determining and pursuing a future direction, for outlining a "means" and a "ways"; pessimism was crippling, hindering all future direction.

Obstructive Sleep Apnea. Like chronic obstructive pulmonary disease, obstructive sleep apnea [OSA] can be debilitating. During sleep, individuals with OSA experience sudden arrests in their breathing, causing them to awake partially and fracturing their rest. This produces profound daytime fatigue and sleepiness, dulls mental acuity, and has been associated with cardiac, vascular, pulmonary, endocrine, and psychiatric dysfunction. Indeed, OSA has been implicated as a risk factor for coronary arterial disease and heart attack.

A study from 2005 concluded that among a population of 4,060 Americans with OSA, 21.8% suffered from depression, 16.7% from anxiety, 11.9% from post-traumatic stress disorder, 5.1% from psychosis, and 3.3% from affective disorders.[74] Two smaller studies attempted to determine the relationship between optimism-pessimism and OSA. On one hand, Aikens *et al* used the Minnesota Multiphasic Personality Inventory in a population of 49 men and women with OSA.[75] They found that compared to age and gender matched controls, individuals with OSA demonstrated more depressive symptoms, including pessimism. On the other hand, Glebocka *et al* used the LOT-R in a population of 63 men and women with OSA.[76] They found no differences in optimism-pessimism between this group and a group of age and gender matched controls.

PESSIMISM AND INGUINAL HERNIA

Approximately 750,000 hernia repairs are performed in the United States.[77] Most of these patients return to work after 2 to 42 days of recovery. This amounts to 10 million days of work – or $37 billion in productivity – lost per year. While there are certainly many factors that contribute to an individual's convalescence following inguinal hernia repair, the role of disposition merits investigation, for some of the variance in length of recovery and time to return to work – that is, the 2 to 42 days – has its origin in the variance of optimism-pessimism.

Bowley *et al* conducted a prospective study of 206 consecutive subjects undergoing elective, unilateral, primary repair of a reducible inguinal hernia. All subjects completed the LOT-R prior to undergoing surgery. Subjects were followed for one year. After their operation, subjects returned to normal activities by a mean of 3 days, and to work by a mean of 21 days. Optimists tended to return to normal activities and to work sooner than pessimists. Interestingly, the authors noted: by and large, surgery in and of itself had very little influence on a patient's recovery. Rather, those who expected a speedy and uneventful recovery actually achieved a speedy and uneventful recovery; those who did not did not. The implications of this study were clear and profound.

PESSIMISM AND OBSTETRICS

Low Birth Weight. The gravid individual experiences many stressors in anticipation of delivery – each prenatal checkup can bring good or bad news. The ability or inability of one to cope with these stressors depends upon disposition. A handful of studies examined the role of optimism-pessimism in pregnancy.

Prenatal maternal stress is a risk factor for premature birth and low birth weight.[78] Lobel *et al* prospectively followed 129 pregnant women, aged from 20 to 43 years, who were registered at a high-risk obstetrics clinic. All subjects completed surveys evaluating demographics, medical histories, health habits, stressors, and dispositions. The authors found that compared to optimists, pessimists were more likely to report higher levels of stress and were also more likely to deliver babies with lower birth weights. Indeed, when the degree of optimism-pessimism was held constant, prenatal maternal stress had no effect on birth outcome. Therefore, the authors concluded: "chronic stress in pregnancy may be a reflection of underlying dispositions that contribute to adverse birth outcomes". In other words, disposition – optimism or pessimism – may have modulated a pregnant woman's levels of stress, which, in turn, ultimately may have influenced birth outcomes. Optimists dealt well with stress and were more likely to have favorable birth outcomes; pessimists dealt poorly with stress and were more likely to have unfavorable birth outcomes. A physiological explanation for this difference was not fully established. However, it may have very well been the case that differences in disposition and birth outcomes were actually reflections of differences in physiology or psychology. For example: poor birth outcome may have been a manifestation of neuroendocrine abnormalities or of tobacco, alcohol, or illicit drug use.

Moreover, compared to optimists, pessimists expressed higher levels of 'parental perception of child vulnerability', a psychological measure of a mother's impressions of a premature infant's risk of physical injury or illness, of a child's fragility.[79] In a study conducted by Allen *et al*, 116 mothers of premature infants completed the LOT, Beck Depression Inventory, General Health Survey, Impact on Family Scale, Medical Outcomes Study Social Support Survey, and the Spielberger State Anxiety Inventory. The authors followed the patients for one year, well after the period during which premature infants were at greatest risk for declines in health. On univariate analysis, Allen *et al* found that compared to optimists, pessimists were more likely to demonstrate high levels of parental perception of child vulnerability, and were, therefore, more likely to seek medical attention and to use healthcare resources for their infants.

Postpartum Blues and Depression. There are both physiological and psychological explanations for the postpartum blues and depression. Physiologists point to the neuroendocrine system, which undergoes significant and sudden changes in the perinatal period. Psychologists point to a pregnant woman's anticipations of birth and motherhood – whether her projections of the future are achieved or not. By this psychological construct, compared to optimists, pessimists would be at reduced risk for postpartum blues or depression – optimists would expect good outcomes, putting themselves at risk for disappointment; pessimists would expect bad outcomes, sheltering themselves from a lack of wish-fulfillment. However, according to a prospective study of 89 pregnant women by Condon and Watson, this was not the case.[80] In fact, the exact opposite was true – "The phenomenology of the blues was not found to be associated with the hypothesized sense of disappointment or anticlimax despite many women's experiences falling short of expectation. Rather, the most powerful predictor of the blues was a sense of pessimism in the late pregnancy which was actually fulfilled by postpartum reality".

PESSIMISM AND GYNECOLOGIC DISORDERS

Two distressing conditions that women face include premenstrual syndrome and urinary incontinence. Perhaps not surprisingly, women with either condition express high levels of pessimism.[81,82]

Ovarian Cancer. Women with a mutation of either the BRCA1 or BRCA2 gene have a 6-63% risk of developing ovarian cancer by the age of 70[83]. Because of this risk – in addition to the fact that the signs and symptoms of this deadly malignancy are often non-specific and subtle –, rigorous surveillance is important. However, this can be a daunting prospect. Indeed, in the setting of a genetic predisposition to a terminal disease, a grim outlook – one tainted by pessimism, hopelessness, and helplessness – does not seems unreasonable.

Ritvo *et al* sought to study this population – 83 patients registered with the Familial Ovarian Cancer Clinic in a large, academic hospital in Toronto, Canada. They sought to determine whether psychological factors influenced a subject's compliance with an established ovarian cancer surveillance regimen. The authors collected data on personal and familial medical histories; performed physical, serological, and radiological examinations; and stratified subjects into low, medium, and high risk groups. Moreover, subjects were asked to complete questionnaires outlining their own perceptions of their levels of risk; their support networks; and their levels of anxiety and worry. Subjects also completed the LOT. The authors considered any patient who unexpectedly missed an annual follow-up appointment as non-adherent. On univariate analysis, the authors found that the only predictor of compliance or noncompliance with an ovarian cancer surveillance regimen was perceived risk – whereas those who perceived themselves to be at low or medium risk of developing ovarian cancer were likely to comply, those who perceived themselves to be at high risk were unlikely to comply. Interestingly, actual risk was not significant. These findings offered an intriguing insight into the psychology of optimists and pessimists – simply: compared to optimists, pessimists were less likely to pursue medical attention because they were haunted by a persistent and overwhelming sense of doom. Therefore, the pessimist, whether or not his or her expectations for the future were supported by reality, acquiesced to what she perceived to be a grim and inevitable future; she accepted her fate.

PESSIMISM AND ENDOCRINE DISORDERS

MEN1 stands for multiple endocrine neoplasia type 1. These patients have a genetic mutation, which puts them at increased risk for pituitary, parathyroid, and pancreatic neoplasms. According to a study of 29 men and women by Berglund *et al*, most patients with MEN1 were pessimists.[84] Moreover, compared to optimists, pessimists were more likely to report poor mental health.

PESSIMISM AND DERMATOLOGICAL DISORDERS

Psoriasis is a chronic dermatological condition that often exhibits a waxing-and-waning clinical course. Because it affects the skin, its cosmetic effects can cause profound distress among patients. A study of 100 men and women with psoriasis by Zalweska *et al* found that optimists were more likely than pessimists to accept and cope with their disease.[85] Age, gender, disease duration and severity, and family history had no effect.

PESSIMISM AND ORTHOPEDIC DISORDERS

Osteoarthritis. Osteoarthritis of the knee – persistent degeneration, or "wear-and-tear", of joint cartilage with formation of new, often misshaped, bone – is one of the indications for knee replacement surgery, particularly in the setting of persistent pain and dysfunction. However, the operative results do not last forever and revision may be required. Venkataramanan studied a population of 184 men and women undergoing revision knee replacement surgery.[86] In addition to a survey of their medical histories, subjects completed the LOT among other batteries. Overall, these subjects – who elected to pursue elective, repeat surgery – were optimistic and believed that their recovery would be uneventful. However, even within this population, compared to optimists, pessimists tended to do more poorly. Other significant factors that delayed recovery were persistent concern over surgery, poor general health, poor past experience with knee replacement, and pain.

Brenes *et al* performed a somewhat related study. They noted that while different patients had similar levels of disease severity, some reported minimal dysfunction and others reported complete dysfunction. [87] The authors sought to explain these findings by determining psychological predictors of physical functioning in a population of 480 ambulatory men and women aged 65 years or older – mean age was 72 years. All subjects reported suffering from and being debilitated by knee pain on most days. X-ray confirmation of the diagnosis and of disease severity were obtained. All subjects were observed completing four simple, daily physical tasks: walking, lifting an object, climbing stairs, and getting into and out of a car. All subjects completed the LOT. The authors found that compared to non-optimists – be they pessimists or not (Brenes *et al* divided the LOT such that it considered optimism and pessimism to be two unipolar entities, rather than two ends of a continuous spectrum) –, optimists did better in the walking task. Moreover, compared to non-pessimists, pessimists did worse in all four of the physical tasks. The only other factors that that were associated with physical function were: African-American race, number of arthritic joints, and disease severity.

These findings were noteworthy for several reasons. First, they again underscored the premise that optimism and pessimism were two independent variables rather than two ends of a continuum. Second, they provided an answer to the question: Why do two people with the same degree of osteoarthritis exhibit different degrees of physical dysfunction? Brenes *et al* posit several possibilities as to why non-optimists and pessimists fared worse than their respective counterparts. Perhaps they were less adroit at coping with the stress and pain of disease. Or: perhaps they were less likely to pursue or comply with interventions, resulting in poorer general health, less physical activity, poorer physical conditioning, and greater disability.

Musculoskeletal Pain. A few studies – examining the relationship between optimism-pessimism and bone and muscle pain – were conducted using very specific study populations: patients with end-stage renal disease,[88] patients with fibromyalgia,[89] and rheumatoid arthritis.[90] According to Devins *et al*, among 100 men and women with end-stage renal disease, compared to optimists, pessimists were more likely to experience persistent and pervasive muscle pain. According to Affleck *et al*, among 89 women with fibromyalgia, compared to optimists, pessimists were more likely to experience limitations in their daily activities due to pain. According to Sinclair, among 90 women with rheumatoid arthritis, compared to optimists, pessimism were more like to report significant psychosocial distress due to pain.

PESSIMISM AND HIV-AIDS

HIV-AIDS Risk. Moyer *et al* studied a group of 101 pregnant women in Ghana; all were HIV-negative and all completed the LOT-R.[91] The authors found that compared to optimistic women, pessimistic women were likely to know more about HIV-AIDS and were more likely to have been tested for serum conversion.

These findings seemed to have complemented earlier work by Perkins *et al*, who evaluated a population of 53 homosexual men in a small city in the American South.[92] All of the subjects were HIV-negative; all provided data on sexual behaviors; and all completed the LOT. The authors divided their study population into three groups based upon self-reports of condom use, numbers of sexual partners, and types of sexual activities: those who engaged in low-risk sexual behavior (60%), those who engaged in moderate-risk sexual behavior (17%), and those who engaged in high-risk sexual behavior (23%). Perkins *et al* found that compared to optimists, pessimists were more likely to practice low-to-moderate-risk sexual behavior.

These two studies seemed to suggest that optimism was associated with enhanced awareness of the risks of contracting HIV, and pessimism was associated with less awareness. Indeed, insofar as HIV-AIDS was concerned, it seemed as though optimism was detrimental, and pessimism was beneficial – though optimism was associated with a certain nonchalance or recklessness, and as though pessimism was associated with insight and caution. Indeed, for these patients, it seemed as though pessimism, not optimism, was protective.

Disease Course. In his study of 412 men and women with HIV-AIDS, J Milam used the term 'post-traumatic growth', which referred to the ability to experience and perceive positive changes following a devastating life event.[93] Milam noted that 59-83% of people who became serum-positive for HIV reported post-traumatic growth. He also noted that subjects who achieved post-traumatic growth demonstrated improved immune functions – that they had enhanced lymphocyte proliferation, increased natural killer cell activity, and, among HIV-positive men, slower rates of decline in CD4 counts. Milam posited that these findings may have been a function of stress hormones – known immune modulators –, particularly cortisol; individuals with higher levels of stress demonstrated higher levels of serum cortisol, and individuals with lower levels of stress demonstrated lower levels of serum cortisol.

Post-traumatic growth could be seen as a measure of coping, of overcoming a significant stressor. Therefore, based upon data from other diseases, it was not unreasonable to assume that optimists would have demonstrated more post-traumatic growth; and pessimists, less. Indeed, this seemed to have been the case. Compared to subjects with high levels of optimism, subjects with low levels of optimism demonstrated an increased positive association between post-traumatic growth and CD4 count – quite simply: the least optimistic individuals reported more post-traumatic growth and higher CD4 counts. Also, Milam found that compared to subjects with high levels of pessimism, subjects with low levels of pessimism demonstrated an increased negative association between post-traumatic growth and serum viral loads – quite simply: the least pessimistic individuals demonstrated the most post-traumatic growth and lower serum viral loads. In other words, for this population, low measures of optimism and pessimism were more beneficial than high measures of optimism and pessimism. These findings seemed to suggest that optimism and pessimism were different entities – two separate unipolar scales, rather than two ends of a bipolar continuum. Moreover, they seemed to suggest that for patients with HIV-AIDS, a temperate disposition – one not overwhelmingly optimistic or pessimistic – may have been more beneficial, or – at the very least – reflective of a more indolent disease course than an extreme disposition. Indeed, it may have been the case that low levels of optimism and pessimism reflected a state that was more open to change, one that was neither persistently overcoming stressors nor persistently overwhelmed by them.

Chemotherapeutic Compliance. Antiretroviral therapy is the mainstay of treatment for patients with HIV-AIDS, and has allowed for patients to live reasonably long and healthy lives. It has converted HIV-AIDS from a terminal illness into a 'lifestyle' illness, one akin to hypertension or diabetes. Because the signs and symptoms of disease may be better controlled and less apparent, patients may be inclined to alter or discontinue therapy without medical guidance.

Aversa and Kimberlin studied the relationship between optimism-pessimism and compliance with antiretroviral therapy in a population of 99 subjects with HIV-AIDS.[94] Unfortunately and disturbingly, only 26% of subjects were compliant with their medications. Not surprisingly, compliers tended to be optimistic about the effects of antiretroviral therapy. Also, interestingly, even though they experienced more symptoms from their disease, they reported having better health – in a sense, they were the most optimistic about health though they were the least healthy. Of the subject population, 36% altered their chemotherapeutic regimens without medical guidance and 37% discontinued their chemotherapeutic regimens altogether without medical guidance. These subjects tended to be more pessimistic both in regard to the benefits of antiretroviral therapy and in general. Therefore, the symptomatic optimist, who could appreciate the signs and symptoms of HIV-AIDS in him or herself and the benefits of treatment, was more likely than the asymptomatic pessimist, who could appreciate neither the implications of infection nor the benefits of treatment.

PESSIMISM AND CANCER

While there have been numerous – somewhat inclusive – studies examining the relationship between various psychological constructs – for example: personality structures, mood, hope, social support, and anger – and cancer, there have been much fewer studies examining the relationship between optimism-pessimism and cancer.

Cancer Risk. J Denollet studied cancer risk in a population of 246 men diagnosed and treated for coronary arterial disease.[95] All men were aged from 31 to 79 years, healthy – except for their diagnosis of heart disease –, active, and free of the signs and symptoms of cancer. At study entry, all subjects completed numerous psychological batteries, including a measure of optimism-pessimism. Subjects were followed for a mean of 7.8 years. Denollet found that 12 subjects (5%) had been diagnosed with and 9 subjects had died of cancer; 3 patients with cancer were still alive. Three subjects were diagnosed with lung cancer, 3 with gastrointestinal cancer, 3 with hematogenous cancer, 2 with prostate cancer, and 1 with colon cancer. Denollet found numerous factors – both psychological and physical – that were associated with the development of cancer: older age, poorer exercise tolerance, and pessimism and anxiety. Denollet did not provide conclusive explanations for these findings. Perhaps pessimists were less likely to pursue routine cancer screening or to seek medical attention even when the signs and symptoms of disease were present. Perhaps they were more likely to smoke tobacco or drink alcohol. Perhaps there were complicated physiological – particularly immune – phenomena that governed the mechanics of the body and the expressions of the mind.

However, as striking as these data were, one must have exercised caution in interpreting them, for despite a somewhat sizable total study population and despite a prospective design, only 12 subjects developed cancer. Moreover, the study population was rather homogenous as it was limited to functional, middle-aged and older, Belgian men with coronary arterial disease. Therefore, while the relationship between pessimism and cancer was shown be statistically significant, Denollet's findings could not have been used for clinical decision-making.

Cancer Mortality. Both folk wisdom and a handful of studies have suggested that a proactive stance towards overcoming cancer was more beneficial in relieving the signs and symptoms of disease and in enhancing survival than a mindset characterized by acceptance, stoicism, hopelessness, and helplessness – that cancer patients with a 'fighting spirit' did better than cancers patients who 'gave-up'.[96,97,98]

Schulz *et al* sought to study this premise, focusing on optimism and pessimism as they relate to cancer mortality.[99] The authors followed 268 men and women with metastatic or recurrent cancers. The most common cancers were breast and lung. All subjects were receiving palliative radiation therapy for the symptoms of disease at the time of study recruitment. Though all subjects were ambulatory and none were enrolled in a hospice program, each subject's life expectancy was estimated to be one year or less. All subjects completed the LOT. At 8-month follow-up, 70 of 238 subjects had died. The authors found that pessimism was associated with an increased risk of mortality among younger patients – patients aged between 30 and 59 years –; however, pessimism was not a risk factor for mortality among patients older than 60 years of age. Moreover, optimism and depression were not associated with cancer mortality. These results reinforced the premise that optimism and pessimism were distinct entities, rather than opposite ends of a spectrum. Also, they demonstrated that the implications of optimism and pessimism were relative – that optimism may have been far superior to pessimism for one population (younger patients), but inconsequential for another population (older patients). Indeed, Schulz *et al* posited that compared to their younger counterparts, older subjects did not necessarily view cancer as an anathema. Therefore, they may have been better able to cope with disease, and may have, in fact, used pessimism as a tool for overcoming the stressors of malignant disease. As such, pessimism was not necessarily a marker of debilitation and disengagement. Compared to the young, for the old, pessimism and disease may have been "more customary".

Thanatology. Several studies have looked at optimism-pessimism and thanatology – the study of death and dying – particularly in caregivers, loved ones, family members, and friends of those with terminal cancers. One study – conducted among a population of 26 partners of patients with advanced gastrointestinal cancers – found that compared to optimists, pessimist exhibited more psychological distress in regard to death.[100] Another study was conducted by Tomarken *et al*.[101] They examined a population of 248 caregivers of patients with terminal cancers. Each subject completed the LOT along with several other psychological batteries. They sought to determine risk factors for complicated grief, which was characterized by "intense yearning, difficulty accepting the death, excessive bitterness, numbness, emptiness, and feeling uneasy" and by the belief that the future was bleak. On multivariate analysis, Tomarken *et al* found that compared to optimists, pessimists were statistically more likely to experience complicated grief. The only other statistically significant factor was the presence of concurrent severe stressors. Statistically non-significant factors included: age, income, history of depression, current depression, and perceived social support. The authors concluded: "These results suggest that mental health professionals who work with caregivers should pay particular attention to pessimistic thinking and stressful life events, beyond the stress of the loved one's illness, that caretakers experience".

PESSIMISM AND HEAD AND NECK CANCERS

Quality of Life. Using different subject populations and different psychological instruments, a few authors have investigated the relationship between optimism-pessimism and quality of life in patients with head and neck cancers. Allison et al used the French version of the LOT in a group of 101 French men and women with recent diagnoses of advanced head and neck cancers.[102] Holloway et al used the Functional Assessment of Cancer Therapy, the Functional Assessment of Cancer Therapy – Head and Neck, the Millon Behavioral Health Inventory, and the Social Support Questionnaire in a group of 105 men and women who had survived 5 years or more after being diagnosed with head and neck cancers.[103] Kung et al used the Minnesota Multiphasic Personality Inventory and the Short-Form Health Survey in a group of 190 men and women who had survived an average of 12.5 years after being diagnosed with head and neck cancers, including thyroid cancers.[104] These studies concluded: overall, compared to optimism, pessimism was associated with poorer quality of life in patients with head and neck cancers; whereas optimists tended to report high levels of physical and psychological well-being, pessimists tended to report low levels. Moreover, as their diseases progressed, pessimists expressed further physiologic and emotional deterioration and distress.

The main limitation of these studies was that they seemed to have stated the obvious: optimists fared better than pessimists. Another question that warranted investigation was perhaps: Did levels of optimism-pessimism differ among subjects with and without head and neck cancers? This was investigated by Llewellyn et al who used the LOT, the Satisfaction with Life Scale, the Hospital Anxiety and Depression Scale, and the Short-Form Health Survey in a group of 162 men and women recently diagnosed with and treated for head and neck cancers.[105] One hundred and fifteen subjects were diagnosed with oral cancer and had undergone radical surgery; 47 subjects were diagnosed with throat cancer and had undergone curative radiation therapy; and 33 subjects were diagnosed with benign salivary conditions and had undergone minor surgeries. The authors begin their report by stating: "It seems reasonable to suppose that a patient treated surgically for cancer of the mouth will have a worse quality and satisfaction with life than the normal population". However, Llewellyn et al found that the three groups – patients with oral cancers, patients with throat cancers, and patients with benign salivary conditions – did not differ in their self-reported measures of optimism or pessimism, and reported similar levels of subjective well-being.

A similar study was conducted by Bjordal et al but arrived at different conclusions.[106] This study evaluated subjective well-being in a population of 204 subjects who had been diagnosed with head and neck cancers 7 to 10 years prior to study enrollment. Bjordal et al found that compared to a group of healthy controls, subjects with head and neck cancers reported worse physical and emotional states.

Possible reasons for differences between these two studies were numerous – both had small study populations; one included subjects who had just undergone surgery and the other included subjects who had survived long-term; one was conducted in Great Britain and the other was conducted in Norway; etc.

Head and Neck Cancer Mortality. Citing work on the relationship between optimism-pessimism and other diseases, particularly other cancers, Allison et al followed a population of 101 French men and women with a mean age of 58.3 years diagnosed with head and neck cancers.[107] Most subjects were diagnosed with advanced disease and treated with multifaceted therapy. All subjects completed the French version of the LOT. At one year follow-up, approximately half of the subject population had died. Controlling for clinical, social, and demographic factors on multivariate analysis, Allison et al found that two factors were associated with one-year mortality in these patients: pessimism and living alone. The odds ratios were 1.12 with a 95% confidence interval of 1.01 to 1.24 and 4.14 with the confidence interval of 1.21 to 14.17 respectively. The authors did not provide conclusive explanations for their findings but postulated that subjects who were more optimistic or who cohabited were better able to cope with the stressors of disease, and that optimism-pessimism may have modulated the immune system. However, Allison et al pointed out that their study population was small and that they did not evaluate performance status, socioeconomic status, smoking status, or biologic markers of prognosis other than cancer stage.

PESSIMISM AND BREAST CANCER

Breast Cancer Screening. Early detection and treatment of breast cancer is associated with improved long-term outcomes, including disease-free and overall survivals.[108] Despite public campaigns to promote breast cancer screening and intervention – and despite the fact that most women who detect a lesion on self-examination present to medical attention within two weeks –, up to 34% of women delay consultation for 3 months or longer. Indeed, approximately 30-50% of new cases of breast cancer in the United States present in later stages.

While lower educational and socioeconomic statuses, lack of health insurance, older age, and being a racial or ethnic minority are known risk factors for delayed presentation, the role of psychosocial variables was unclear. Mohamed et al studied the relationship between several psychological measures, including optimism-pessimism, and delayed presentation of breast cancer. They utilized several psychological instruments: the LOT, Body Investment Scale, Hospital Anxiety and Depression Scale, Monitor-Blunter Style Scale, Multidimensional Health Locus of Control Scale, and Religious Coping Scale. The results were perhaps a bit surprising: "The hypotheses that women with locally-advanced breast cancer would demonstrate increased levels of anxiety, blunting, and external locus of control were not confirmed using psychometric data". Indeed, no significant psychological differences were found between women who presented with late-stage breast cancer and women who presented with early-stage breast cancer. Not unexpectedly, however, delayed presentation was associated with inattention to routine breast cancer screening, denial, fatalism, and reliance on alternative therapies. (It must be emphasized: this study utilized an exceedingly small study population, and therefore, while its results were interesting and noteworthy, no broader clinical conclusions could have been drawn.)

Quality of Life in Breast Cancer. Though breast cancer is not as lethal as lung, pancreatic, or ovarian cancers, the implications of diagnosis are not minor. A diagnosis of breast cancer threatens a woman's physical and psychological identities. It is not without distress. Therefore, much of the work on optimism-pessimism and breast cancer has focused on women's abilities to accept, to cope, and to overcome the stressors of diagnosis, treatment, and recovery.

Montgomery et al studied the relationship between optimism-pessimism and the perioperative period for women with breast cancer.[109] Indeed, whether a woman underwent diagnostic or therapeutic surgery; lumpectomy or mastectomy; no lymph node biopsy, sentinel lymph node biopsy, or axillary dissection; no reconstruction or reconstruction, the perioperative period was a stressful one. The authors followed a group of 61 women with a mean age of 52 years and a range of ages from 22 to 77 years who presented to one of two breast surgeons at a large, urban, academic medical center. For this study, all women underwent lumpectomy under local sedation and monitoring with either diagnostic or therapeutic intent. All women completed the LOT prior to surgery. Though their study population was small, Montgomery et al achieved some rather interesting and notable results. Information provided by the surgeon prior to surgery – whether the surgery was for diagnosis or treatment, the benefits and risks of surgery, the likelihood of cancer – did not influence the amount of distress a women felt. Indeed, the only significant factors were: preoperative optimism-pessimism, worry about the surgery and anesthesia, and worry about the operative findings. Perhaps this was not surprising insofar as optimism and pessimism were expressions of expectations for the future – optimists expected good things to happen to them and pessimists expected bad things to happen to them.

For women with known or suspected breast cancer, as stressful as the preoperative period is, the postoperative period may be just as or even more stressful. In addition to the physical and emotional stressors of having gone through surgery and anesthesia, of confronting a new body image, of nursing an operative wound, this is the period during which a woman awaits the surgical pathological results. This is the period during which tumor size, lymph node involvement, and metastatic spread – id est: the period during which breast cancer stage and prognosis – are determined. Schou et al sought to determine whether a woman's disposition changed during this period, whether after receiving good or bad news, an optimist remained an optimist or a pessimist remained a pessimist.[110] The authors recruited 165 women who were diagnosed with breast cancer and presented for a surgical consultation. All subjects completed the LOT-R at the time of diagnosis, and at 3 and 12 months following surgery. Perhaps insofar as optimism-pessimism was a personality construct and therefore presumed stable across situation and time, the results were not surprising: Schou et al found that despite receiving good or bad news, individual dispositions did not change from diagnosis to 3 months following surgery, or from diagnosis to 12 months following surgery. Of course, it could have been the case that the diagnosis of breast cancer itself may have altered a woman's disposition such that no further news – good or bad – could have produced any alterations to her level of optimism-pessimism – that after the overwhelming shock of being diagnosed with breast cancer, further shocks were seemingly comparatively minor.

The bulk of the work on optimism-pessimism and breast cancer deals with the ability of women to adjust to and to cope with the diagnosis. C Carver et al note: "the diagnosis of breast cancer is threatening on many levels. The patient's life is threatened by the disease, the surgical treatment is disfiguring, and there are also secondary threats to the woman's social and emotional well-being (e.g., fear of being stigmatized when people learn of the diagnosis, worry over whether the cancer has spread, uncertainly about the future of one's children if the cancer does not respond to treatment, and financial issues). Given this wide range of repercussions, the diagnosis of breast cancer represents a serious crisis in the lives of the women diagnosed".[111] Whereas some women respond well to the diagnosis, some women do not.

Numerous studies have sought to determine whether optimism-pessimism could predict such adjustment or maladjustment. Two studies were conducted by Carver et al in women with early stage breast cancer.[112] One included 59 subjects and the other 70 subjects. At study enrollment, optimism-pessimism was measured using the LOT. One day prior to surgery, 10 days following surgery, and at 3, 6, and 12 months following surgery, subjects reported their levels of psychological adjustment, coping, and distress. Other studies were conducted by Schou et al.[113,114] They followed 165 women; utilized the LOT; recorded adjustment, coping, and distress; and followed patients for 1 year. Despite some differences between the works of Carver et al and Schou et al – for example: one was conducted in the United others, and the other was conducted in Norway; one was conducted in the era of minimally disfiguring surgery, and the other was conducted in the era of modified radical mastectomies –, by and large, they arrived at largely similar results. Quite simply: compared to optimists, pessimists fared worse at all points from diagnosis, to surgery, to follow-up. Optimists were more likely to report having a "fighting spirit", and expressed adjustment, good coping, and low levels of distress; pessimists were more likely to report hopelessness and helplessness, and expressed maladjustment, poor coping, and high levels of distress. In their earlier work, Schou et al found that pessimism was clearly a risk factor for both anxiety and depression following surgery. For anxiety and depression, odds ratios were 0.86 with a 95% confidence interval of 0.77-0.95, and 0.83 with a 95% confidence interval of 0.73-0.95 respectively. Interestingly, however, Carver et al noted that both optimists and pessimists reported, similar modest levels of interference of their daily lives from pain. Also, both groups reported minimal changes in their sex lives.

These trends seemed to translate to other realms of the life of a woman with breast cancer. Three studies examined the relationship between optimism-pessimism and return to work, social engagement and isolation, and participation in support groups among patients with breast cancer. First, Hakanen and Lindbohm demonstrated that compared to optimists, pessimists were less able to engage in work.[115] Moreover, optimists were better than pessimists in dealing with a stressful work environment. Second, Carver et al concluded what compared to optimists, pessimists were less likely to engage in social and recreational activities at the time of diagnosis and at one year thereafter.[116] The authors also noted that compared to optimists, pessimists were more likely to be distressed and fatigued. This may – in part – have provided an explanation for the social engagement of the former group and the social isolation of the latter. Third, Schou et al found that compared to optimists, pessimists were less likely to participate in a support group intended for survivors of breast cancer.[117] The odds ratio was 0.89 with a 95% confidence interval of 0.83-0.98. Compared to the group of subjects that did not participate in the support group, the group of subjects that did participate demonstrated a substantial reduction in rates of anxiety.

IV: WHAT ARE THE BIOLOGY AND CHEMISTRY OF OPTIMISM-PESSIMISM?

Some of the research into the biological and chemical underpinnings of optimism-pessimism has already been described – particularly in regard to the pathologic physiology of cardiac and vascular disorders, of HIV-AIDS, and of cancer. Here, further works are discussed, organized by scientific discipline.

Anatomy. Most of the research into the anatomy of optimism-pessimism has utilized Positron Emission Tomography, or PET Scanning. One such work was conducted by Fischer *et al.*[118] He and his colleagues asked 13 healthy female subjects to view videotaped images of snakes while undergoing PET Scanning of their brains. Moreover, they were asked to describe the images. These responses were evaluated for level of optimism-pessimism using the Attributional Style Questionnaire. Fischer *et al* found that compared to optimists, pessimists exhibited decreased activity of the right and left amygdalas, deep and ancient regions of the brain previously described as modulators of emotions and memories.

These findings seemed to have been supported by a work by Sharot *et al.*[119] The authors begin their report rather provocatively: "Humans expect positive events in the future even when there is no evidence to support such expectations. For example, people expect to live longer and be healthier than average, they underestimate their likelihood of getting a divorce, and overestimate their prospects for success on the job market". Like Fischer *et al*, Sharot *et al* demonstrated: compared to when subjects imagined pessimistic scenarios, when subjects imagined optimistic scenarios, the amygdala and rostral anterior cingulate cortex – another portion of the brain implicated in cognition, decision-making, emotion, memory, and planning – demonstrated enhanced activity. Moreover, the authors noted that dysfunction of these areas was associated with depression, which often included a persistent and pervasive sense of pessimism. It was perhaps not surprising that the part of the brain responsible for optimism-pessimism would have also been responsible for cognition, decision-making, emotion, memory, and planning. Indeed, the projection of future events must have certainly represented the most executive of executive functions, one capable of evaluating and integrating all aspects of an experience.

Cellular Physiology. Cortisol is a stress hormone produced by the adrenal gland with effects throughout the body – it influences the effects of insulin; carbohydrate, protein, and fat metabolism; electrolyte metabolism; vascular capacitance and resistance – that is: blood pressure –; gastric acid production and secretion; immune function; bone metabolism; and even learning and memory. Therefore, Lai *et al* sought to research the relationship between optimism-pessimism and cortisol. The authors recruited 80 healthy men and women living in Hong Kong. All subjects completed the Chinese version of the LOT at study enrollment and provided 12 samples of saliva over a course of 2 days. For each specimen, salivary cortisol levels were determined. Lai *et al* found that compared to optimists, pessimists displayed higher levels of cortisol during daytime hours. However, optimists and pessimists displayed similar levels of cortisol during nighttime hours. Differences were more pronounced in women than in men. This made sense: because cortisol was a stress hormone, one would have expected to find low levels of it in optimists, who could have easily overcame stress; and one would have expected to find high levels of it in pessimists, who could have easily been overwhelmed by stress.

The relationship between optimism-pessimism and immune function was previously discussed. In short: compared to optimists, pessimists have decreased lymphocyte proliferation, decreased natural killer cell activity, and, among HIV-positive men, faster rates of decline in CD4 counts. Moreover, these may be the result of the neuroendocrine effects of increased levels of stress hormones seen in those with lower levels of optimism and higher levels of pessimism. One study demonstrated these findings among HIV-positive back women.[120] Indeed, in a population of 36 African-American, Haitian, and Caribbean women with HIV-AIDS, compared to optimists, pessimists demonstrated lower activity of natural-killer cells and T-cells. In other words, they had poorer cellular immune function, placing them at increased risk for immune-compromise and the risks thereof, including AIDS-defining illnesses, and cervical dysplasia and cancer.

Molecular Biology. Monoamine oxidase inhibitors [MAOIs] and tricyclic antidepressants [TCAs] are two classes of medicine available for the pharmacological treatment of depression. However, they seem to have different effects: while patients with depression report improvement whether they are on

MAOIs or TCAs, those on the former report less pessimistic sentiments than those on the latter.[121] Therefore, it stands to reason that MAOIs are better able to target the molecular modulators of pessimism – at least in patients with depression – than TCAs are. It also stands to reason that variations in these targets – or their corresponding neurotransmitters and/or associated proteins – may account for some of the variations present in optimism-pessimism – again: at least in patients with depression.

A handful of studies have investigated these possibilities. One concluded that variations in two dopamine receptors – D2 and D4 – may account for variations in adaptability and coping, affect, sociability, and well-being or distress.[122] Another study found that a base-pair deletion in the genetic sequence for a serotonin gene promoter accounted for some of variation in optimism-pessimism – optimists were more likely to have the base-pair deletion; pessimists were more likely not to have the base-pair deletion.[123]

CONCLUSIONS

The present work has attempted to provide an overview of the psychology of pessimism, focusing and organizing the discussion around four questions: I: How are optimism and pessimism measured?, II: What is the relationship between optimism and pessimism?, III: What is the relationship between optimism-pessimism and health?, and IV: What are the biology and chemistry of optimism-pessimism?

Throughout these pages and even within these four questions themselves, the insightful reader will have noted an interesting phenomenon: despite the fact that its authors have attempted to focus as much as possible on pessimism, the present work is as much as a work on optimism as it is a work on pessimism. Perhaps this is inevitable – especially if, as has been assumed for the greater part of the history of psychology, optimism and pessimism represent two ends of a continuum of human disposition. However, as seen, current research suggests that this is not the case. Optimism and pessimism are, in fact, probably two separate entities.

Or: perhaps the inseparability of optimism and pessimism represents something else. Perhaps it reflects the unshakable belief that optimism is good and pessimism is bad. And just as good and bad are inseparable, perhaps optimism and pessimism are inseparable too – even if psychological data suggest otherwise.

The complexity of the relationship between optimism and pessimism make this point painfully clear: further research is needed. The present work has posed four questions – I: How are optimism and pessimism measured?, II: What is the relationship between optimism and pessimism?, III: What is the relationship between optimism-pessimism and health?, and IV: What are the biology and chemistry of optimism-pessimism? Surely, there are further questions to be asked and further answers to be determined.

REFERENCES

[1]   American Psychiatric Association. *Diagnostic and Statistical Manual of Mental Disorders, Fourth Edition, Text Revision.* Washington, DC, American Psychiatric Association. 2000.

[2]   Beck AT, Weissman A, Lester D, Trexler L. The measure of pessimism: the hopelessness scale. *Journal of Consulting and Clinical Psychology* 1974; 42: 861-865.

[3]   Fibel B, Hale WD. The generalized expectancy scale for success scale – a new measure. *Journal of Consulting and Clinical Psychology* 1978; 46: 924-931.

[4]   Hale WD, Fiedler LR, Cochran CD. The revised expectancy for success scale: a validity and reliability study. *Journal of Clinical Psychology* 1992; 48: 517-521.

[5]   Scheier MF, Carver CS. Optimism, coping, and health: assessment and implications of generalized outcome expectancies. *Health Psychology* 1985; 4: 219-247.

[6]   Smith TW, Pope MK, Rhodewalt F, Poulton JL. Optimism, neuroticism, coping, and symptom reports: an alternative interpretation of the life orientation test. *Journal of Personality and Social Psychology* 1989; 4: 640-648.

[7]   Scheier MF, Carver CS, Bridges MW. Distinguishing optimism from neuroticism (and trait anxiety, self-mastery, and self-esteem): a reevaluation of the life orientation test. *Journal of Personality and Social Psychology* 1994; 67: 1063-1078.

[8]   Dember WN, Martin SH, Hummer MK, Howe SR, Melton RS. The measurement of optimism and pessimism. *Current Psychology: Research and Reviews* 1989; 8: 102-119.

[9]   Chang EC, D'Zurilla TJ, Maydeu-Olivares A. Assessing the dimensionality of optimism and pessimism using a multimeasure approach. *Cognitive Therapy and Research* 1994; 18: 143-160.

[10] Snyder CR, Harris C, Anderson JR, Holleran SA, Irving LM, Sigmon ST, Yoshinobu L, Gibb J, Langelle C, Harney P, The will and the ways: development and validation of an individual–differences measure of hope. *Journal of Personality and Social Psychology* 1991; 60: 570-585.

[11] Peterson C, Semmel A, von Baeyer C, Abramson LY, Metalsky GI, Seligman MEP. The attributional style questionnaire. *Cognitive Therapy and Research* 1982; 6: 287-299.

[12] Peterson C, Schulman P, Castellon C, Seligman MEP. The explanatory style scoring manual. In Smith CP, editor. *Handbook of Thematic Analysis.* New York: Cambridge University Press. 1992.

[13] Herzberg PY; Glaesmer H, Hoyer J. Separating optimism and pessimism: a robust psychometric analysis of the revised life orientation test (LOT-R). *Psychological Assessment* 2006; 18: 433-438.

[14] Mroczek DK, Sprio A, Aldwin CM, Ozer DJ, Bossé R. Construct validation of optimism and pessimism in older men: findings from the Normative Aging Study. *Health Psychology* 1993; 12: 406-409.

[15] Robinson-Whelen S, Kim C, MacCullum RC, Kiecolt-Glaser JK. Distinguishing optimism from pessimism in older adults: is it more important to be optimistic or not to be pessimistic? *Journal of Personality and Social Psychology* 1997; 73: 1345-1353.

[16] Räikkönen K, Matthews KA. Do dispositional pessimism and optimism predict ambulatory blood pressure during school days and nights in adolescents? *Journal of Personality* 2008; 76: 605-630.

[17] Robbins AS, Spence JT, Clark H. Psychological determinants of health and performance: the tangled web of desirable and undesirable characteristics. *Journal of Personality and Social Psychology* 1991; 61: 755-765.

[18] Maruta T, Colligan RC, Malinchoc M, Offord KP. Optimists versus pessimists: survival rate among medical patients over a 30 year period. *Mayo Clinic Proceedings* 2000; 75: 140-143.

[19] Maruta T, Colligan RC, Malinchoc M, Offord KP. Optimism-pessimism assessed in the 1960s and self-reported health status 30 years later. *Mayo Clinic Proceedings* 2002; 77: 748-753.

[20] Peterson C, Seligman MEP, Vaillant GE. Pessimistic explanatory style is a risk factor for physical illness: a thirty-year longitudinal study. *Journal of Personality and Social Psychology* 1988; 55: 23-27.

[21] Achat H, Kawacki I, Spiro A, DeMolles DA, Sparrow D. Optimism and depression as predictors of physical and mental health functioning: the Normative Aging Study. *Annals of Behavioral Medicine* 2000; 22: 127-130.

[22] Steptoe A, Wright C, Kunz-Ebrecht SR, Iliffe S. Dispositional optimism and health behavior in community-dwelling older people: associations with health aging. *British Journal of Health Psychology* 2006; 11: 71-84.

[23] Steptoe A, O'Donnell K, Marmot M, Wardle J. Positive affect and psychological processes related to health. *British Journal of Psychology* 2008; 99: 211-217.

[24] Ruthig JC, Allery A. Native American elders' health congruence: the role of gender and corresponding functional well-being, hospital admissions, and social engagement. *Journal of Health Psychology* 2008; 13: 1072-1081.

[25] Scioli A, Chamberlin CM, Samor CM, Lapointe AB, Campbell TL, Macleod AR, Mclenon J. A prospective study of hope, optimism, and health. *Psychological Reports* 1997; 81: 723-733.

[26] Ruthig JC, Chipperfield JG, Perry RP, Newall NE, Swift A. Comparative risk and perceived control: implications for psychological and physical well-being among older adults. *Journal of Social Psychology* 2007; 147: 345-369.

[27] Umstattd MR, McAuley E, Motl RW, Rosengren KS. Pessimism and physical functioning in older women: influence of self-efficacy. *Journal of Behavioral Medicine* 2007; 30: 107-14.

[28] Carvajal SC, Evans RI, Nash SG, Getz JG. Global positive expectancies of the self and adolescents' substance use avoidance: testing a social influence meditational model. *Journal of Personality* 2002; 70: 421-442.

[29] Taylor WC, Baranowski T, Klesges LM, Ey S, Pratt C, Rochon J, Zhou A. Psychometric properties of optimism and pessimism: results from the Girls' Health Enrichment Multisite Studies. *Preventative Medicine* 2004; 38: 69-77.

[30] Kelloniemi H, Ek E, Laitinen J. Optimism, dietary habits, body mass index and smoking among young Finnish adults. *Appetite* 2005; 45: 169-176.

[31] Fontaine KR, Cheskin LJ. Optimism and obesity treatment outcomes. *Journal of Clinical Psychology* 1999; 55: 141-143.

[32] Costello BA, McLeod TG, Locke GR, Dierkhising RA, Offord KP, Colligan RC. Pessimism and hostility scores as predictors of patient satisfaction ratings by medical out-patients. *International Journal of Health Care Quality Assurance* 2008; 21: 39-49.

[33] Auerbach SM, Kiesler DJ, Wartella J, Rausch S, Ward KR, Ivatury R. Optimism, satisfaction with needs met, interpersonal perceptions of the healthcare team, and emotional distress in patients' family members during critical care hospitalizations. *American Journal of Critical Care* 2005; 14: 202-210.

[34] Ylöstalo P, Ek E, Knuuttila M. Coping and optimism in relation to dental health behavior – a study among Finnish young adults. *European Journal of Oral Sciences* 2003; 111: 477-483.

[35] Ylöstalo P, Sakki T, Jarvelin M-R, Knuuttila M. Dental check-ups in 31-year-olds in relation to optimism and life satisfaction. *Community Dental Health* 2005; 22: 106-112.

[36] Wardle J. Dental pessimism: negative cognitions in fearful dental patients. *Behavior Research and Therapy* 1984; 22: 553-556.

[37] Tomberg T, Toomela A, Ennok M, Tikk A. Coping strategies, social support, life orientation and health-related quality of life following traumatic brain injury. *Brain Injury* 2005; 19: 1181-1190.

[38] Tomberg T, Toomela A, Ennok M, Tikk A. Changes in coping strategies, social support, optimism, and health-related quality of life following traumatic brain injury: a longitudinal study. *Brain Injury* 2007; 21: 479-488.

[39] Hermann BP, Trenerry MR, Colligan RC. Learned helplessness, attributional style, and depression in epilepsy. *Epilepsia* 1996; 37: 680-686.

[40] Watten VP, Watten RG. Psychological profiles in patients with medically refractory epilepsy. *Seizure* 1999; 8: 304-309.

[41] Hart SL, Vella L, Mohr DC. Relationships among depressive symptoms, benefit-finding, optimism, and positive affect in multiple sclerosis patients after psychotherapy for depression. *Health Psychology* 2008; 27: 230-238.

[42] Jønsson A, Dock J, Ravnborg MH. Quality of life as a measure of rehabilitation outcome in patients with multiple sclerosis. *Acta Neurologica Scandinavica* 1996; 93: 229-235.

[43] Slaughter JR, Slaughter KA, Nichols D, Holmes SE, Martens MP. Prevalence, clinical manifestations, etiology, and treatment of depression in Parkinson's disease. *Journal of Neuropsychiatry and Clinical Neurosciences* 2001; 13: 187-196.

[44] Lyons KS, Stewart BJ, Archbold PG, Carter JH, Perrin NA. Pessimism and optimism as early warning signs for compromised health for caregivers of patients with Parkinson's Disease. *Nursing Research* 2004; 53: 354-362.

[45] Sipila K, Ylostalo PV, Ek E, Zitting P, Knuuttila ML. Association between optimism and self-reported facial pain. *Acta Odontologica Scandinavica* 2006; 64: 177-182.

[46] Costello NL, Bragdon EE, Light KC, Sigurdsson A, Bunting S, Grewen K, Maixner W. Temporomandibular disorder and optimism: relationships to ischemic pain sensitivity and interleukin-6. *Pain* 2002; 100: 99-110.

[47] Lamontagne LL, Hepworth JT, Salisbury MH, Riley LP. Optimism, anxiety, and coping in parents of children hospitalized for spinal surgery. *Applied Nursing Research* 2003; 16: 228-235.

[48] Labbe EE, Lopez I, Murphy L, O'Brien C. Optimism and psychological functioning for children with Batten's and other neurological disorders. *Psychological Reports* 2002; 90; 1129-1135.

[49] Barron CR, Foxall MJ, von Dollen K, Shull KA, Jones PA. Loneliness in low-vision older women. *Issues in Mental Health Nursing* 1992; 13: 387-401.

[50] Scott B, Lindberg P, Melin L, Lyttkens L. Control and dispositional style among the hearing-impaired in communication situations. *Audiology* 1994; 33: 177-184.

[51] Räikkönen K, Matthews KA, Flory JD, Owens JF, Gump BB. Effects of optimism, pessimism, and trait anxiety on ambulatory blood pressure and mood during everyday life. *Journal of Personality and Social Psychology* 1999; 76: 104-113.

[52] Grewen K, Girdler SS, West SG, Bragdon E, Costello N, Light KC. Stable pessimistic attributions interact with socioeconomic status to influence blood pressure and vulnerability to hypertension. *Journal of Women's Health and Gender-Based Medicine* 2000; 9: 905-915.

[53] Nabi H, Vahtera J, Singh-Manoux A, Pentti J, Oksanen T, Gimeno D, Elovaino M, Virtanen M, Klaukka T, Kivimaki M. Do psychological attributes matter for adherence to antihypertensive medication? The Finnish Public Sector Cohort Study. *Journal of Hypertension* 2008; 26: 2236-2243.

[54] Rosengren A, Hawken S, Ôunpuu S, Sliwa K, Zubaid M, Almahmeed WA, Blackett KN, Sitthi-Amorn C, Sato H, Yusuf S. Association of psychosocial risk factors with risk of acute myocardial infarction in 11,119 cases and 13,648 controls from 52 countries (the INTERHEART Study): case-control study. *The Lancet* 2004; 364: 953-962.

[55] Kuper H, Marmot M. Systemic review of prospective cohort studies of psychosocial factors in the etiology and prognosis of coronary heart disease. *Seminars in Vascular Medicine* 2002; 2: 267-314.

[56] Bunker SJ, Colquhoun DM, Esler MD, Hickie IB, Hunt D, Jelinek VM, Oldenburg BF, Peach HG, Ruth D, Tennant CC, Tonkin AM. "Stress" and coronary heart disease: psychosocial risk factors. *The Medical Journal of Australia* 2003; 178: 272-276.

[57] Kubzansky LD, Sparrow D, Vokonas P, Kawachi I. Is the glass half empty or half full? A prospective study of optimism and coronary heart disease in the Normative Aging Study. *Psychosomatic Medicine* 2001; 63: 910-916.

[58] Todaro JF, Shen B-J, Niaura R, Spiro A, Ward KD. Effect of negative emotions on frequency of coronary heart disease (The Normative Aging Study). *The American Journal of Cardiology* 2003; 92: 901-906.

[59] Giltay EJ, Geleijnse JM, Zitman FG, Hoekstra T, Schouten EG. Dispositional optimism and all-cause and cardiovascular mortality in a prospective cohort of elderly Dutch men and women. *Archives of General Psychiatry* 2004; 61: 1126-1135.

[60] Everson SA, Kaplan GA, Goldberg DE, Salonen R, Salonen JT. Hopelessness and 4-year progression of carotid atherosclerosis. *Arteriosclerosis, Thrombosis, and Vascular Biology* 1997; 17: 1490-1495.

[61] Matthews KA, Räikkönen K, Sutton-Tyrrell K, Kuller LH. Optimistic attitudes protect against progression of carotid atherosclerosis in healthy middle-aged women. *Psychosomatic Medicine* 2004; 66: 640-646.

[62] Rozanski A, Blumenthal JA, Kaplan J. Impact of psychological factors in the pathogenesis of cardiovascular disease and implications for therapy. *Circulation* 1999; 99: 2192-2217.

[63]   Wiklund I, Sanne H, Vedin A, Wilhelmsson C. Psychosocial outcome one year after a first myocardial infarction. *Journal of Psychosomatic Research* 1984; 28: 309-321.

[64]   Brink E, Grankvist G. Associations between depression, fatigue, and life orientation in myocardial infarction patients. *Journal of Cardiovascular Nursing* 2006; 21: 407-411.

[65]   Gulliksson M, Burell G, Lundin L, Toss H, Svärdsudd K. Psychosocial factors during the first year after a coronary heart disease event in cases and referents. Secondary Prevention in Uppsala Primary Health Care Project (SUPRIM). *BMC Cardiovascular Disorders* 2007; 7: 36-44.

[66]   Halpin LS, Barnett SD. Preoperative state of mind among patients undergoing CABG: effect on length of stay and postoperative complications. *Journal of Nursing Care Quality* 2005; 20: 73-80.

[67]   Scheier MF, Matthews KA, Owens JF, Magovern GJ, Lefebvre RC, Abbott RA, Carver CS. Dispositional optimism and recovery from coronary artery bypass surgery: the beneficial effects on physical and psychological well-being. *Journal of Personality and Social Psychology* 1989; 57: 1024-1040.

[68]   Scheier MF, Matthews KA, Owens JF, Schulz R, Bridges MW, Magovern GJ, Carver CS. Optimism and rehospitalization after coronary artery bypass graft surgery. *Archives of Internal Medicine* 1999; 159: 829-835.

[69]   Rowe MA, King KB. Long-term chest wall discomfort in women after coronary artery bypass grafting. *Heart and Lung* 1998; 27: 184-188.

[70]   Ben-Zur H, Rappaport B, Ammar R, Uretzky G. Coping strategies, life style changes, and pessimism after open-heart surgery. *Health and Social Work* 2000; 25: 201-209.

[71]   Kubzansky LD, Wright RJ, Cohen S, Weiss S, Rosner B, Sparrow D. Breathing easy: a prospective study of optimism and pulmonary function in the Normative Aging Study. *Annals of Behavioral Medicine* 2002; 24: 345-353.

[72]   Chronic obstructive pulmonary disease (COPD) fact sheet. American Lung Association. Available at: http://www.lungusa.org/site/pp.asp?c=dvLUK9O0Eandb=35020. Accessed July 5, 2006.

[73]   Alberto J, Joyner B. Hope, optimism, and self-care among Better Breathers Support Group members with chronic obstructive pulmonary disease. *Applied Nursing Research* 2008; 21: 212-217.

[74]   Sharafkhaneh A, Giray N, Richardson P, Young T, Hirshkowitz M. Association of psychiatric disorders and sleep apnea in a large cohort. *Sleep* 2005; 28: 1405-1411.

[75]   Aikens JE, Mendelson WB. A matched comparison of MMPI responses in patients with primary snoring or obstructive sleep apnea. *Sleep* 1999; 22: 355-359.

[76] Glebocka A, Kossowska A, Bednarek M. Obstructive sleep apnea and the quality of life. *Journal of Physiology and Pharmacology* 2006; 57: 111-117.

[77] Bowley DMG, Butler M, Shaw S, Kingsnorth AN. Dispositional pessimism predicts delayed return to normal activities after inguinal hernia operation. *Surgery* 2003; 133: 141-146.

[78] Lobel M, DeVincent CJ, Kaminer A, Meyer BA. The impact of prenatal maternal stress and optimistic disposition on birth outcomes in medically high-risk women. *Health Psychology* 2000; 19: 544-553.

[79] Allen EC, Manuel JC, Legault C, Naughton MJ, Pivor C, O'Shea TM. Perception of child vulnerability among mothers of former premature infants. *Pediatrics* 2004; 113: 267-273.

[80] Condon JT, Watson TL. The maternity blues: exploration of a psychological hypothesis. *Acta Psychiatrica Scandinavica* 1987; 76: 164-171.

[81] Keenan PA, Lindamer LA, Jong SK. Psychological aspects of premenstrual syndrome: Utility of standardized measures. *Psychoneuroendocrinology* 1992; 17: 189-194.

[82] Walters MD, Taylor S, Schoenfeld LS. Psychosexual study of women with detrusor instability. *Obstetrics and Gynecology* 1990; 75: 22-26.

[83] Rivto R, Irvine J, Robinson G, Brown L, Murphy KJ, Matthew A, Rosen B. Psychological adjustment to familial-genetic risk assessment for ovarian cancer: predictors of nonadherence to surveillance recommendations. *Gynecologic Oncology* 2002; 84: 82-80.

[84] Berglund G, Lidén A, Hansson MG, Öberg K, Sjöden PO, Nordin K. Quality of life in patients with multiple endocrine neoplasia type 1 (MEN1). *Familial Cancer* 2003; 2: 27-33.

[85] Zalewska A, Miniszewska J, Chodkiewicz J, Narbutt J. Acceptance of chronic illness in psoriasis vulgaris patients. *Journal of the European Academy of Dermatology and Venereology* 2007; 21: 235-242.

[86] Venkataramanan V, Gignac MA, Mahomed NN, Davis AM. Expectations of recovery from revision knee replacement. *Arthritis and Rheumatism* 2006; 55: 314-321.

[87] Brenes GA, Rapp SR, Rejeski WJ, Miller ME. Do optimism and pessimism predict physical function? *Journal of Behavioral Medicine* 2002; 25: 219-231.

[88] Devins GM, Armstrong SJ, Mandin H, Paul LC, Hons RB, Burgess ED, Taub K, Schorr S, Letourneau PK, Buckle S. Recurrent pain, illness intrusiveness, and quality of life in end-stage renal disease. *Pain* 1990; 42: 279-285.

[89] Affleck G, Tennen H, Zautra A, Urrows S, Abeles M, Karoly P. Women's pursuit of personal goals in daily life with fibromyalgia: a value-expectancy analysis. *Journal of Consulting and Clinical Psychology* 2001; 69: 587-596.

[90] Sinclair VG. Predictors of pain catastrophizing in women with rheumatoid arthritis. *Archives of Psychiatric Nursing* 2001; 15: 279-288.

[91]   Moyer CA, Ekpo G, Calhoun CL, Greene J, Naik S, Sippola E, Stern DT, Adanu RM, Koranteng IO, Kwawukume EY, Anderson FJ. Quality of life, optimism-pessimism, and knowledge and attitudes toward HIV screening among pregnant women in Ghana. *Women's Health Issues* 2008; 18: 301-309.

[92]   Perkins DO, Leserman J, Murphy C, Evans DL. Psychosocial predictors of high-risk sexual behavior among HIV-negative homosexual men. *AIDS Education and Prevention* 1993; 5: 141-152.

[93]   Milam J. Postraumatic growth and HIV disease progression. *Journal of Consulting and Clinical Psychology* 2006; 74: 817-827.

[94]   Aversa SL, Kimberlin C. Psychosocial aspects of antiretroviral medication use among HIV patients. *Patient Education and Counseling* 1996; 29: 207-219.

[95]   Denollet J. Personality and risk of cancer in men with coronary heart disease. *Psychological Medicine* 1998; 28: 991-995.

[96]   Greer S, Morris T, Pettingale KW. Psychological response to breast cancer: effect on outcome. *The Lancet* 1979; 2: 785-787.

[97]   Greer S. Psychological response to cancer and survival. *Psychological Medicine* 1991; 21: 43-49.

[98]   Phillips DP, Todd ER, Wagner LM. Psychology and survival. *The Lancet* 1993; 342: 1142-1145.

[99]   Schulz R, Bookwala J, Knapp JE, Scheier M, Williamson GM. Pessimism, age, and cancer mortality. *Psychology and Aging* 1996; 11: 304-309.

[100]   Winterling J, Wasteson E, Sidenvall B, Sidenvall E, Glimelius B, Sjoden P-O, Nordin K. Relevance of philosophy of life and optimism for psychological distress among individuals where death is approaching. *Supportive Care in Cancer* 2006; 14: 310-319.

[101]   Tomarken A, Holland J, Schachter S, Vanderwerker L, Zuckerman E, Nelson C, Coups E, Ramirez PM, Prigerson H. Factors of complicated grief pre-death in caregivers of cancer patients. *Psycho-Oncology* 2008; 17: 105-111.

[102]   Allison PJ, Guichard C, Gilain L. A prospective investigation of dispositional optimism as a predictor of health-related quality of life in head and neck cancer patients. *Quality of Life Research* 2000; 9: 951-960.

[103]   Holloway RL, Hellewell JL Marbella AM, Layde PM, Myers KB, Campbell BH. Psychosocial effects in long-term head and neck cancer survivors. *Head and Neck* 2005; 27: 281-288.

[104]   Kung S, Rummans TA, Colligan RC, Clark MM, Sloan JA, Novotny PJ, Huntington JL. Association of optimism-pessimism with quality of life in patients with head and neck and thyroid cancers. *Mayo Clinic Proceedings* 2006; 81: 1545-1552.

[105] Llewellyn CD, Weinman J, McGurk M. A cross-sectional comparison of cognitive and emotional well-being in oral cancer patients. *Oral Oncology* 208; 44: 124-132.

[106] Bjordal K, Mastekaasa A, Kaasa S. Self-reported satisfaction with life and physical health in long-term cancer survivors and a matched control group. *European Journal of Cancer* 1994; 31: 340-345.

[107] Allison PJ, Guichard C, Fung K, Gilain L. Dispositional optimism predicts survival status 1 year after diagnosis in head and neck cancer patients. *Journal of Clinical Oncology* 2003; 21: 543-548.

[108] Mohamed IE, Skeel-Williams K, Tamburrino M, Wryobeck J, Carter Sue. Understanding locally advanced breast cancer: what influences a woman's decision to delay treatment? *Preventative Medicine* 2005; 41: 399-405.

[109] Montgomery GH, David D, Goldfarb AB, Silverstein JH, Weltz CR, Birk JS, Bovbjerg DH. Sources of anticipatory distress among breast surgery patients. *Journal of Behavioral Medicine* 2003; 26: 153-164.

[110] Schou I, Ekeberg Ø, Sandvik L, Ruland CM. Stability in optimism-pessimism in relation to bad news: a study of women with breast cancer. *Journal of Personality Assessment* 205; 84: 148-154.

[111] Carver CS, Pozo-Kaderman C, Harris SD, Noriega V, Scheier MF, Robinson DS, Ketcham AS, Moffat FL, Clark KC. Optimism versus pessimism predicts the quality of women's adjustment to early stage breast cancer. *Cancer* 1994; 73: 1213-1220.

[112] Carver CS, Pozo C, Harris SD, Noriega V, Scheier MF, Robinson DS, Ketcham AS, Moffat FL, Clark KC. How coping mediates the effect of optimism on distress: a study of women with early stage breast cancer. *Journal of Personality and Social Psychology* 1993; 65: 375-390.

[113] Schou I, Ekeberg Ø, Ruland CM, Sandvik L, Karensen R. Pessimism as a predictor of emotional morbidity one year after following breast surgery. *Psycho-Oncology* 2004; 13: 309-320.

[114] Schou I, Ekeberg Ø, Ruland CM. The mediating role of appraisal and coping in the relationship between optimism-pessimism and quality of life. *Psycho-Oncology* 2005; 14: 718-727.

[115] Hakanen JJ, Lindbohm M-L. Work engagement among breast cancer survivors and the referents: the importance of optimism and social recourses at work. *Journal of Cancer Survivorship* 2008; 2: 283-295.

[116] Carver CS, Lehman JM, Antoni MH. Dispositional pessimism predicts illness-related disruption of social and recreational activities among breast cancer patients. *Journal of Personality and Social Psychology* 2003; 84: 813-821.

[117] Schou I, Ekeberg Ø, Karensen R, Sorensen E. Psychosocial intervention as a component of routine breast cancer care – who participates and does it help? *Psycho-Oncology* 2008; 17: 716-720.

[118] Fischer H, Tillfors M, Furmark T, Fredrikson M. Dispositional pessimism and amygdala activity: a PET study in healthy volunteers. *Neuroreport* 2001; 12: 1635-1638.

[119] Sharot T, Riccardi AM, Raio CM, Phelps EA. Neural mechanisms mediating optimism bias. *Nature* 2007; 450: 102-105.

[120] Byrnes DM, Antoni MH, Goodkin K, Efantis-Potter J, Asthana D, Simon T, Munajj J, Ironson G, Fletcher MA. Stressful events, pessimism, natural killer cell cytotoxicity, and cytotoxic/suppressor T cells in HIV+ black women at risk for cervical cancer. *Psychosomatic Medicine* 1998; 60: 714-722.

[121] Shawcross CR, Tyrer P. Influence of personality on response to monoamine oxidase inhibitors and tricylic antidepressants. *Journal of Psychiatric Research* 1985; 19: 557-562.

[122] Hill SY, Zezza N, Wipprecht G, Locke J, Neiswanger K. Personality traits and dopamine receptors (D2 and D4): linkage studies in families of alcoholics. *American Journal of Medical Genetics* 1999; 88: 634-641.

[123] Samochowiec J, Rybakowski F, Czerski P, Zakrzewska M, Stepien G, Pelka-Wysiecka J, Horodnicki J, Pybakowski JK, Hauser J. Polymorphisms in the dopamine, serotonin, and norepinephrine transporter genes and their relationships to temperamental dimensions measured by the Temperament and Character Inventory in healthy volunteers. *Neuropsychobiology* 2001; 43: 248-253.

INDEX

T